It all began with Moses

J. V. Smith

DEDICATION

To the old families of Nympsfield with whom my family has been connected by marriage over a period of four hundred years prior to the Great War of 1914–1918.

Copyright © 1999 by J. V. Smith

All rights reserved. No part of this publication may be reproduced or transmitted in any form or by any means, electronic or mechanical including photocopying, recording or any information storage or retrieval system, without prior permission in writing from the publishers.

First published by The Choir Press in 1999

The moral right of the author has been asserted

ISBN 0 9535913 0 1

Printed and bound in Great Britain by
Action Publishing Technology Ltd, Gloucester GL1 1SP

Contents

Introduction	1
What's in a Name?	3
Why Nympsfield?	6
Why There?	9
Early Days	11
The Romans	18
The Earliest Christian Community at Nympsfield	24
From Roman to Norman: The First Millennium	27
Pre-Reformation Gloucestershire: The Seeds of Capitalism are sown	32
The Old Families of Nympsfield	36
A Story from the Civil War	42
St. Bartholomew's Church and the Older Buildings of Nympsfield	44
The Revival of Roman Catholicism	48
Woodchester Park	54
Lest We Forget	58
To be a Farmer's Boy: A Job from Dawn to Dusk	60
It has to be like with like	66
Sheep, Wool, and Cloth: A Staple Industry	70
The Bristol and Gloucestershire Gliding Club	76
The Parish Pump	78
The Village Today	80
Appendices	85
Selected Bibliography	88

ACKNOWLEDGEMENTS

I thank all those many friends and relations who have helped and encouraged me, especially my cousins Leslie Cordwell-Smith, a retired architect living in Brighton, and Enid Williams, of Chargy Hill Farm, Maisemore.

Thanks also to the staff of the Records Office in Gloucester, and the City Library in Brunswick Road, Gloucester; the staff of the public libraries at Stroud and Nailsworth, all of whom have been courteous, friendly and helpful in spite of constant questioning.

For specific subjects I thank Jack Marshall, formerly managing director Marling & Evans at Kingstanley and Ebley, who guided me through my researches into the cloth trade; to Major Goldingham for his knowledge of Uley Bury and the Temple of Mercury both on his land, and for allowing me to photograph and reproduce the bust of Mercury in his home, a copy of the original now in the British Museum; to the Rev. Curwen Rawlinson, now retired from active service, who volunteered as the former Rector of Uley, Nympsfield and Owlpen to come back and dedicate the special memorial tombstone to those of my family hitherto unrecorded at St. Bartholomew's Church, Nympsfield; to Sheila Dennison for her great knowledge of Nympsfield, and copious notes freely offered; to John Evans for his enthusiasm and help with the history of Woodchester Park and the Ducie family; to Eddie Price and his son Arthur at Frocester Court Farm; to Margie Ashton for her help with the Daniels family history; the Rev. Fr. Jones-Frank at Woodchester, and the Rev. Fr. Edwin Gordon at Nympsfield.

My special thanks to Professor Owen Chadwick O.M. of Selwyn College, Cambridge, who readily agreed to check over a large section of my draft, sent back pages of alterations and corrections, and encouraged me with his enthusiastic and prompt response to rewrite a number of pages.

Last but not least to Michael Watts of Sheepcote Farm, Nympsfield, who because of his name in history, and ability to mend Cotswold stone roofs, earned the nickname of Watts Tyler. He and his wife Tessa, became my link with the village and the litmus paper to test my ideas.

Introduction

Thomas Carlyle called the historical researcher 'Dryasdust' and when I announced to my family at large that I was going to do a family tree, there were the usual sceptical comments from some, but mostly there was encouragement; Dryasdust seemed a good nickname.

It was when I began to visit the Records Office and local libraries that I found others doing precisely the same thing. For weeks on end I delved into books both old and new – around seventy altogether – looked at photographs and maps, and asked many questions of staff, friends and relations, and came up with a mass of names and dates. Some of it was unrelated and some unintelligible, and sadly much of it was put on one side for I am easily sidetracked: yet it was not a waste of time because each book and each scrap of information was like a tube of oil paint to an artist and helped to add colour to my scene.

In the end, given that all the facts are the same, a different historian would compile a different story and this one just happens to be mine.

As for Dryasdust it became for me the wrong nickname altogether. I realised that amongst all the names and dates were the human lives and tragedies of my forebears set amidst a sea of similar biographies in the Cotswold upland village of Nympsfield, and in the district around. There were direct links with Stroud, Dursley, Berkeley, Nailsworth, Uley, Wotton under Edge, Stonehouse, Frocester, the two Stanleys, Owlpen, Ebley and Woodchester. It would be Dryasdust simply to draw up a family tree and leave it at that.

So the story I have to tell is not just about a family named Smith. It is the story about Nympsfield and the villages around: of the people who lived and worked there.

Nympsfield is an isolated and bypassed Cotswold village, but it is also very English. Gloucestershire folk might call it 'the back of beyond'. Let them recall that when the Rev Grice was inducted as Vicar of Gransden near Cambridge he was told that 'Great Gransden is the end of the world, and Little Gransden is a quarter of a mile beyond it.'

Visiting Nympsfield today you would be excused if a similar thought entered your head.

So this introduction will end with a quote from a delightful poem written by C. H. Towne called 'The best road of all'.

> I like a road that leads away to prospects bright and fair
> A road that is an ordered road, like a nun's evening prayer
> But best of all I love a road that leads to God knows where.

He knows where it is and so do I. For me it is a very special place.

What's in a Name?

It was a family joke. If anyone asked about the history of the Smith family, the cry would go up, 'It all began with Moses'.

We knew it didn't. That was unrealistic and impractical. We knew something had happened before Moses, but as with the biblical character it was a good starting point.

It was only when you stopped saying the response, that you had to ask yourself if it was worth looking further and finding what else there was to know.

When a fellow born John Smith begins to ask questions about his past he is faced with an Everest to climb, a planet to explore. In my case I was greatly helped by the fact that my paternal great grandfather was named Moses. The name stands out like a sore thumb or a jewel in the crown according to your opinion or choice. There was no previous use of the Christian name in our family, and none after. Moses stood alone.

Why Richard and Mary Smith should have chosen the name Moses for their second son born in 1819 will never be known now. Their first child was a boy named John, a most reasonable first name; but then I am biased.

Moses conjures up bullrushes and baskets, and the man who led the Israelites out of Egypt, and divided the waters of the Red Sea. That Moses was born in Egypt, and Moses is a name commonly found on the Nile. In Egyptian, Moses means simply 'boy' or 'son' and is written as MS for there are no vowels in hieroglyphics. Those who prefer not to use the title 'Mrs' or 'Miss' and have adopted 'Ms' will no doubt take due note.

The baptismal records of St. Bartholomew's Church, are resonant with sounds of the most beautiful and poetic Christian names: Temperance (Townsend) Angelica (Daniels) Philadelphia (Howell) Letitia, or Lettice (Howell) Priscilla (Mills) Swindonia (Shelton). You will also find Isobella, Georgina, and a repetition of Harriets, Mary Anns (nicknamed Polly) Hannahs, Marthas and Charlottes; not forgetting the boys Jehoshophat (Daniels) and of course Moses (Smith).

Some names are repeated regularly within families and this can be a guide pointing to a family connection but it can be a great disadvantage when you find three different Benjamin Mills in the village at one and the same time. My maternal great great grandfather was Joseph Mills, but in the same period between 1813 and 1818 there were two other Joseph Mills, and all three are in the baptismal records as fathers.

It is therefore easy to see in the Mills family, as in any other, why someone would refer to 'our Joseph' or 'our Benjamin' as opposed to the boy next door, or in another branch of the same family.

Names are also repeated within a family when a child dies, so frequently the case in the early nineteenth century and before. A later born child would then be given the deceased child's name so that the name would remain alive and be retained within the family.

Moses Smith had an older brother, John, who died in infancy, and so the third born, also a boy, was given the name John.

On the distaff side, my great grandfather William Mills born in 1816, was the second son born to Joseph and Hester Mills and given the name William, the first born William having died in infancy.

Similarly when my great grandfather Moses and his wife Mary Ann (Bushell) became parents their first three children died young. They had been named Moses, David, and Charles. In this case the first to die was Charles, and then a girl was born named Harriet. The fifth child was a boy and he was given the name Charles to keep that name alive. This was my grandfather Charles Smith. The other two children of Moses and Mary Ann Smith were girls and so there was no chance to repeat Moses and David. A great grandson of Moses, and my cousin, was given the name David, but by then the climate for biblical names in Christian families was passing.

Moses was never repeated. He became the first in the family and doubtless the last.

In what sort of a place did Moses Smith get raised and bring up his own family? Who were his forebears and what did they do to make a living, and keep body and soul together? Why did they live in Nympsfield? Why did they stay there? What was the great attraction?

Why Nympsfield?

The basic questions to be asked about any place, no matter how large or small, are twofold. The first question to be answered is how and why did it get its name and the second question to be answered is why is it situated where it is?

The English Place Names Society stated that Nympsfield comes from an old British Celtic word Nymed implying that it is a field or tract of land belonging to one called Nymed. This suggests that Nymed might be a personal name; or it is a shrine, a holy place. There is strong evidence for both theories, and there is also a third theory which more recent apologists, with an early rush of political correctness, have discarded as being less romantic, and to which I will return.

The shrine or holy place is readily understandable for there are three famous burial grounds within shouting distance of the village at Coaley Peak (the Long Barrow at the Picnic Site), the Soldiers Grave nearby in the quarry in Buckholt Wood, and the finest of all at Hetty Pegler's Tump between Nympsfield and Uley Bury. At Woodchester Park, Bown Hill, Selsley Hill and Nailsworth there are other barrows not too far away, and beneath the central development of the village itself lies a further barrow recorded by its name alone. Opposite Hetty Pegler's Tump and within the last two decades there has been the remarkable and accidental discovery of a Roman Temple to Mercury later converted to a Christian establishment. So the Society may well be right in that theory.

As for the idea that Nymed is a personal name from Celtic times, I have no comment, except that the earliest reference in writing to Nympsfield comes in an annal of 862 AD which was later published in the Anglo Saxon Chronicle which gives a clue in the language from that part of Europe. In that annal the words 'im Nimdesfelda' appear. 'Im' translates in the later German to 'in the', and 'des' to 'of the' or 'some'. This would, by that reasoning, give 'in the fields of Nim' and line up with the personal name theory.

Now I return to my less fashionable, less romantic, and so far discarded theory that again derives from the old German where 'nehmen' means 'to take' and 'nimm' is the imperfect form. Margaret Drabble in The Oxford Companion to English Literature tells us that 'to nym or to nim' is slang for 'to steal'.

From this viewpoint 'im Nimdesfelda' would mean 'theft of the fields' or just the Stolen Fields, or the field of the thief.

Those who know their Shakespeare will readily recognise the character Nym; Corporal Nym, friend and follower of Falstaff along with Lieutenant Bardolph and Pistol. Nym appears in 'The Merry Wives of Windsor' and in 'Henry V', and Drabble refers to him as a rogue and a thief, obsessed with humours.

His partners were a similar pair; Pistol the braggart and Bardolph the red-nosed rogue who is hanged just before Agincourt for stealing from a French church.

Shakespeare did have connections with this part of Gloucestershire. It is in Henry IV Part 2 that Justice Shallow's servant Davy says to his master

'I beseech you, sir, to countenance William Visor of Wincot ...'

Those who know the Gloucestershire accent especially as you move through the south of the county and into Bristol itself, will know that there is a tradition of cutting words short. It is a lazy habit but amongst local folk it is both widespread and acceptable. Woodmancote on the outskirts of Dursley would have been pronounced in the abbreviated form of 'Woncot or Wincot'. In neighbouring Cam churchyard there is a tombstone to an Arthur Vizar who died in 1620, and was bailiff of Dursley in 1612. Shakespeare died in 1616 so they would have been contemporaries.

In Richard the Second, Act 2 Scene 3, Bolingbroke asks

> 'How far is it to Berkeley now, my lord?'

to which Northumberland replies

> 'I am a stranger here in Glostershire: these high wild hills and rough uneven ways,
>   Draw out our miles and make them wearisome'

and shortly afterwards, Bolingbroke asks

> 'How far is it to Berkeley?'

to which Percy replies

> 'There stands the castle, by yond tuft of trees'

The scene of Berkeley Castle in those days would have come from many points on the Cotswold ridgeway but Stinchcombe Hill stands above Dursley and is the most likely. There is a Shakespeare Walk in Dursley, and a Thomas Shakespeare was married there in 1678. The bard undoubtedly knew his Gloucestershire, and was skilled at including local names and tales to widen interest.

What evidence is there for stolen fields?

Nympsfield is situated at the joining point of three hundreds and was, over its long history, part of more than one manor. In the ninth century a dispute occurred over ownership of the Woodchester estate of which Nympsfield was for so long a part along with Berkeley. The estate had been described in a charter between 716 and 745 and was part of a grant of King Aethelbald, but the landmarks were in dispute. Was this how it got its name?

Later the romantics got to work and added 'ph' to the title and it was spelt Nymphsfield. I have found it spelt that way from 1755, but that gives an entirely different meaning to the name and should not be supported.

When my grandparents Charles Smith and his wife Jane (Mills) both died in 1921, their Death Certificates were marked 'born at Nymphsfield', but they had left the village forty-five years earlier and were buried in Ebley.

Why There?

To answer this we must delve into prehistory and look at those who first inhabited the area.

Between Selsley Hill and Uley Bury, a distance of under four miles, there are at least seven known tumuli. As with all existing barrows, they were built near the tracks in everyday use. They were sited on high ground, so that the souls of the chieftains of the community could oversee affairs after death, and also because the high ground meant they were nearer heaven. In the case of these seven barrows they were all close to the Cotswold ridgeway and so commanded splendid views.

Recent excavations at the top of Crawley Hill and opposite Hetty Pegler's Tump have revealed a large community, suggesting that apart from those who were living within the fortifications of Uley Bury, the present village of Nympsfield did not exist during those years. When the Romans came to the district in the first century AD they built or developed the road system between Gloucester and Bath. This may have been as late as 119–122 AD when the Fosse Way was extended beyond Cirencester to Bath and Exeter. The road climbed up the steep 45° escarpment from Frocester and zigzagged to what we now call Coaley Peak. From there it went south for half a mile, and where the old tinkers track was crossed there was developed the present village site.

Now I must confess that this is pure speculation but what adds to the strength of my theory is that the tinker's track, now called Tinkley Lane, that comes from Nailsworth via Forest Green, went in a straight line from the present

Nympsfield Cross in a westerly direction and joined the ancient Cotswold ridgeway near Uley Bury just where the recent archaeological dig took place.

At that time there would have been no call for a settlement where Nympsfield now is, but after the successful Roman invasion there would have been every need to move to the present site, at the crossing place of two important roads.

Frocester also provides us with another example of how a village can move because of what we would now call market forces. Here we have at the George Inn (happily now restored to its old title) the first hostelry and coach stop on the old Gloucester–Bath road where horses were changed and a fresh team harnessed for the steep climb up the Cotswold escarpment to Nympsfield. This was the part of the journey that in 1698 a lady travelling between the two cities on horseback wrote 'came to Nympsfield after having ascended a very steep and stony hill ten mile to Nympsfield, all bad way.'

At the village of Frocester was the first turnpike on that journey; a Court house, a Manor house, and a chapel at ease. The original Church built on an old burial site was half way between Frocester and Coaley, but as with Nympsfield the later developments were demanded elsewhere. The original church is now demolished and the stone used in the rebuilding of Wycliffe College chapel. It was built on the site of a Roman villa and a burial ground, but as the inhabitants moved away so did the need for a village settlement disappear, and Frocester like Nympsfield is now by its cross roads.

Early Days

The richness of the archaeological discoveries to which I have referred, are of such importance that it would be wrong to move on without reporting them with some detail.

Starting at the most northerly end of the neighbourhood there is the Toots which is a long barrow in two mounded parts and 240' long. It is a double burial chamber with a central depression between the two high points, and to which visual appearance it owes its modest name. There has been a suggestion that Toots derives from Tentates, the Chaldean name for Mercury, and the discovery of a bust to Mercury at the Roman Temple near Uley Bury on Major Goldingham's land may add strength to that theory.

As you stand on the Toots looking north and west, there is an unsurpassed view deep into Wales, to the Black Mountains and the Brecon Beacons, to May Hill, and to the Malverns in Worcestershire. On a clear day you can see into ten counties. There may be some views as good, but none better.

Sir Percival Marling makes this claim in his biography 'Rifleman and Hussar', but that was from his home Stanley Hall; the view from the hill above must be finer.

It was also thought that the Toots was the site of a temple and used by the Druids, the priests and teachers of the Iron Age Celts. They believed in human sacrifices – mostly criminals were used, but if villains were hard to come by, then innocent victims were used. By pure coincidence I trust, it has become the present day site for building beacons to celebrate important occasions, and massive bonfires have been lit in my lifetime to celebrate the coronations of 1937 and 1952.

Marjorie Martyn wrote a poem about the Toots part of which said –

> 'I walk alone where many fires were kindled
> And unafraid I pass the sacred ring;
> I see the mound where still the lords are lying...'

At Bown Hill the long barrow is no longer accessible, and the round barrow on the Woodchester Park estate is now largely destroyed. It was one of about two hundred round barrows on the Cotswolds, and when excavated it revealed a beaker dating from some time during the Bronze Age.

In the centre of Nympsfield village there is a mound now neatly grassed over and built on in part, which was another burial site and retains to this day the name of The Barrow.

Then we come to the three treasures of the area; Hetty Pegler's Tump, the Coaley Peak Long Barrow, and the Soldier's Grave.

Hetty Pegler's Tump is half way between Nympsfield and Uley at the top of Crawley Hill. It is one of about fifty long barrows on the Cotswolds, and V. Grinsell in his book 'The Ancient Burial Grounds of England' considers it to be the finest of the fifty. It is 120' long, 85' wide and 10' high. It was first excavated in 1821 by a local doctor who unearthed thirty skeletons and two stone axes. They appear to have disappeared and rumour has it that his old teaching hospital in London was the beneficiary.

In 1854 it was officially excavated and recorded.

It is thought that Hetty Pegler was the wife of Captain Pegler who lived at Wresden, and there is a tablet in Uley Church to Hester Pegler who died in 1694 and that would line up with the tradition that Captain Pegler fought in the Civil War and especially with the sieges of Bristol and Gloucester in 1643.

Why the tumulus should have been named after his wife is not known. Perhaps he had died and it was named after her as the widow and owner of the land at some time. It is now owned, along with Uley Bury, by Major Goldingham, but a family of Peglers still live and farm in Nympsfield.

Moving north a few hundred yards we come to what is now called Coaley Peak Picnic Site. Coaley, down in the Severn valley beneath this site is an immediate neighbour, and much to the consternation and disapproval of Nimpies, as the good people of Nympsfield are sometimes called, an attempt was made in the 1720s to unite the two parishes. A petition was drawn up and despatched to the Bishop of Gloucester, and there it all ended, for having broken away from Frocester there was no wish to join with Coaley. The edge of Buckholt Wood, the entrance gates to Woodchester Park, and the point where the road from Stroud to Dursley joins the minor road from Nympsfield is of historic importance as it marks the place where the boundaries of the three hundreds of Berkeley, Whitstone, and Longtree meet. There was also the Turnpike House or Gate at the top of the Frocester Hill on the old Roman road from Gloucester to Bath, and the old Cotswold stone turnpike is still there, perhaps altered little since it was last used over two hundred years ago. I find it difficult to follow why it has been named Peak and not Pike but that is a digression, for here too is a chambered long barrow which has been tidied up, its covering removed and stones reset to encourage inspection.

It was excavated in 1937 by Mrs E. M. Clifford, and it is recorded that sixteen human skeletons were found, along with pottery and a flint leaf arrowhead now in the Stroud Museum.

Directly opposite Hetty Pegler's Tump is the recently excavated Roman site where a bust of Mercury was discovered which is now in the British Museum in London.

Many relics and coins were unearthed and it is considered that here was a temple to Mercury, the god of merchants and merchandise, and also the fleet-footed and presumably mercurial messenger of the gods. He is commonly identified with the Greek god, Hermes, and his mother Maia, for certainly both Mercury and Maia share the same festival day of May 15th.

For those who argue the case for Nympsfield's origin being a shrine or holy place, the discovery of this temple on top of all the other relics provides support. At the same time it should be remembered that Hermes, the Mercury of the Greek tradition was also a known thief with a smooth tongue and nimble brain and so was also the god of prudence, cunning and theft: even in this example each side can find supporting evidence.

The temple had its birth in the Iron Age perhaps, but Mercury was popular with the Romans, for a temple to the god was built in Rome and dedicated on May 15th, 495 BC. There is also the east-west alignment suggesting that here too was a Christian building probably rebuilt in the fifth century after the Roman withdrawal between 410 and 446.

This would support the opinion that although there is ample evidence that followers of the primitive Christian church existed throughout the Roman colonisation of Britain, the main support was for the old gods such as Mercury. If we look in the New Testament to Acts 14.12 where Paul was journeying in Asia Minor he was mistaken for Hermes in disguise such was his skill in debate and eloquence. The story emphasises the respect and strength of worship for the god Hermes at the time which has been dated between 46 and 48 AD, and the use of the Greek god Hermes not the Roman god Mercury should not pass unnoticed. Paul was on a tour away from the Jewish homeland and preaching to the unconverted Gentiles of Asia Minor where the Greek tradition was strongest.

Last but not least was The Soldier's Grave, excavated also by Mrs Clifford in 1937 but now sadly no more. Situated only 230 yards north of the Coaley Peak long barrow in a quarry it was a stone boat-shaped grave giving clear evidence of a belief in an after-life which would have been reached by a lengthy sea journey. It was 56' in diameter with a squared keel and pointed prow 11' long. In the boat were the skeletons of twenty-eight unburnt individuals interred in the late Bronze age tradition, somewhere between 2000 and 1200 BC. Since 1937 it has disappeared, ravaged by quarrying, souvenir hunters, and the natural effects of the weather.

To have had such a number of tumuli and of such quality in so small an area around Nympsfield emphasises its importance in pre-Christian days.

One of the problems with giving dates and periods in history is that time becomes meaningless if you merely reel off the facts.

When you read that the dinosaur lived sixty-five million years ago it doesn't register until you start to break it down.

When we are about to celebrate the second millennium and 2000 years since the birth of Jesus of Nazareth it seems so far back in time. If you multiply that period of 2000 years by 32,500 you will only then have reached the lifetime of the dinosaur and it begins to become more impressive; even frightening.

With the advent of carbon dating and the discoveries of a great deal of new information over a whole range of studies, it becomes apparent that many prehistoric events took place over a much longer period of time than once imagined.

One cannot therefore, be overconfident about dates and times in pre-history, except to the extent of making reasonable guesses and giving overall periods in which events can have happened.

With some hesitation we can suggest that the humans from the Stone Ages (Palaeolithic and Mesolithic) existed before 4000 BC, and were the hunters and nomads of mankind.

They were followed by the members of the new Stone Age (Neolithic) who were the first farmers and arrived from Europe as we now know it around 4000 BC and lasted around 2000 years until roughly 2500–1700 BC.

Then began the Bronze Age until about 750–600 BC with the arrival of Iron Age people, the builders of hill forts, the invading tribes from Europe we put under the generic title of Celts.

The Romans were the next to arrive, first with an aborted invasion in 55 BC and another a year later in 54 BC but they did not stay, except perhaps to trade. Nearly a century passed before the highly successful invasion of 43 AD under the orders of the Emperor Claudius, which led to 400 years of Roman colonialism.

At Uley Bury at 823 feet above sea level, towering over the picturesque village of Uley, and covering an area of 14.5 hectares, or just over 36 acres (the owner says it is only 30 acres) is one of the finest pre-historic Iron Age forts, and a popular place for visitors. It is just over one mile to walk around it and well worth the effort, for it provides a splendid view of the southern Cotswolds, looking down on Cam Long Down, and Dursley. Again much of its glory, the different angle into Wales from that at Selsley or Coaley Peak, is spoiled by the unrestricted natural growth of the weed ash, so that you must walk the full mile to get a clear westerly view.

The flat top of Uley Bury is regularly under plough farmed by the Goldinghams and over the years many Roman coins have been unearthed, and interestingly, as proof that the Roman took over an existing fortification and developed it for its own purposes, a number of gold coins of Belgic Dobunni tribes of Celts have also been found.

It is easy to understand from the size of this hill fort and its geography, the claim that Uley Bury was the Aldershot of the Roman invasion, post 43 AD.

There is an old saying 'scratch Gloucestershire and find Rome' and the Price family at Frocester Court farm will certainly bear that out, but when Michael Watts was building Sheepcote on the Tinkley Lane and digging a drainage trench he came across the skeleton of an adult lying on its left side, and buried in a shallow pit covered by a large single stone. This was in the late 1960s and when the local archaeologist Capt. H.S. Gracie of Amberley was called in for his opinion, he noted a small piece of pottery which he considered to have been contemporary with the body, and dated it all to early Iron Age which would place it between 500 and 600 BC and of the same time as the building of Uley Bury. Of interest also is the fact that it was possible some 2500 years later to state that the adult person was a 'healthy young male of about 20–30 years of age, and with a good set of teeth'.

Nowadays as we look at this hill fort, we can only marvel at the ingenuity and enormous physical effort at its creation. No bulldozers and mechanical grabs then. They built by sheer hard labour and sweat, and with home made tools we would consider today to be inferior, a double line of earthen ramparts and two ditches that have stood the test of time and still invite admiration.

The reference I have made to sweated labour would not have been far from the truth, for the Celts and the Romans both employed slaves. One of the best known examples from the Roman period was the man later to become St. Patrick, the patron Saint of Ireland. Captured by Irish Celtic tribesmen in one of their frequent raids across the Irish Sea he was taken to the Emerald Isle as a slave, escaped and returned to his native

Wales, and then bravely returned as a missionary.

One puzzle about Nympsfield and Uley and all the other hill communities which has exercised me greatly is the question of water. It had to be there in considerable and regularly available quantity. Dowsing is an ancient skill and may well have been used to decide where wells should be dug, but those who have tried it on the Cotswolds shake their heads when asked.

The answer must be that what we call the spring level is much higher in some places. Wells Road in Bisley, the Thames Head sources of the River Thames, Wells Road in Minchinhampton, are such places which leap to mind. I think that Nympsfield is another place with a high water table, and in support of the claim is the siting of Kinley Priory, and the knowledge that there is a spring at the site of the Rose & Crown in the centre of the village which bubbles in steady stream through the cellars to this day. Another point to remember is that beer was brewed in Nympsfield and cloth was woven and felted there from the middle ages, and these trades could not have operated without ready access to water.

Finally we should realise that until the land enclosures in the second half of the eighteenth century, one third of England was under forest, and in consequence the rainfall was double what it is today.

Before we leave the Ancient Britons we should record that these Iron Age men were a trousered race of wine-drinking, pork-eating warriors, users of slings and arrows. They were farmers and brought with them from continental Europe the heavy-wheeled waggon.

The end of these Iron Age Celts also saw the end of centuries in which the Smiths had periods in time named after their skills. Those who worked in gold, silver, bronze, copper, tin, brass, and iron still designed and forged objects of utility and beauty, and used their skills of invention to forward man's advance, but in future the city state and the organised invader would provide the titles. The Stone Age, the Bronze Age, and the Iron Age were over. We were now to refer to a thousand years divided into ages according to the names of the invaders: the Romans, the Saxons, the Danes, and the Normans.

The Romans

With the arrival of the Romans and the extension of their Empire what we now call Gloucestershire grew rapidly in importance.

Their first reconnaissance in 55 BC was brief, as was their next, one year later. Nearly a century passed and then in 43 AD they came to stay and colonise. Over four hundred years went by until in 446 AD the last links with the Roman Empire were broken. The military garrisons had been withdrawn by 410 AD, but it is fair to say that for four hundred years, Britain was a part of the Roman Empire and under direct Roman rule.

As we prepare to hand over our currency and give up what sovereign powers remain, merging with mainland Europe dominated from its geographical centre in Germany, it might be worthwhile casting our minds back over the past four centuries.

That takes us back to the end of the Golden Age of the first Elizabethan era. Just over half way back and we had the Seven Years War (1756–63) which saw the real beginning of the British Empire. That Empire lasted barely two hundred years, and that puts into perspective the success of the Roman invasion of this island.

I emphasise 'this island' for the Romans did not bother to cross the Irish Sea. My father-in-law, George Lee who was County Engineer (formerly County Surveyor) for County Galway used to say he greatly regretted the fact the Romans did not go to Ireland. 'It would have made my job a lot easier if they had come,' he remarked.

For the first forty years until just after 80 AD the Roman Second Legion was stationed at Gloucester, the lowest crossing point to ford the River Severn. Then after the defeat of the Silures from South Wales between 74 and 78 AD, the military line was advanced to Caerleon, and there had been no need for a military base at Cirencester since 60 AD.

Cirencester throughout this period was the second largest town in England after London. It reached its peak under Diocletian in the fourth century, and became the provincial capital of one of the four Roman governors of Britain, Britannia Prima; the other three were London, York, and Lincoln. Its population was in excess of 5000 but by the end of the second century, the population of all England, admittedly difficult to ascertain with any certainty, was estimated at only around one and half million. To put the population figures into further perspective, by the early Tudor period in the late fifteenth century, it had only just doubled to around three millions, and by the 1801 Census it had reached eight millions. In the half century or so since World War II, the population of the United Kingdom increased by over ten millions to around 57 millions, thirty-eight times larger than mid-way through the Roman conquest of these islands.

The importance to Nympsfield of Roman stewardship was that here was the provincial capital just fifteen miles away; the Second Legion at Gloucester thirteen miles to the north at the fording of the River Severn at its lowest point; and the reserves in camp on the doorstep at Uley Bury and possibly Selsley Hill. As time went by, the main road from Gloucester to Bath was built straight through Nympsfield, and two major villas, one believed to have been for the Provincial Governor, were built within two miles either side of the village at Woodchester and at Frocester. These must have been busy and exciting times for the locals.

Woodchester villa, containing the largest and most elaborate Roman mosaic so far discovered anywhere outside Italy, is a village in itself, which is not surprising for the two words village and villa have the same root.

The mosaic is about forty-six feet square in a room about fifty feet square, just one of a known sixty rooms in the villa, which covers an area almost the size of three football pitches placed side by side; 200 yards by 120 yards.

Wentworth Woodhouse, the largest privately owned stately home in Britain in modern times, is of similar frontage.

The mosaic is of enormous historical importance; it is invaluable and irreplaceable. That it should be buried for ever because of the problems its opening would create for the organisers, particularly in parking vehicles, is a sad reflection on modern ability and ingenuity. When one sees what money is available through the National Lottery, and the annual surplus created from the Road Fund Licence I can only shake my head in disbelief.

The villa was first built as a more modest farm around 120 AD and then was remodelled and greatly extended in 284 AD. Later building between 350–370 is also recorded but shortly afterwards it was destroyed by fire.

Nor is this Woodchester site important for its unique Roman villa alone for on part of the villa is the site of a priory built for Earl Godwin's wife, the Countess Gytha before 1050, but more of that later.

To refer only to the Roman invasion in military terms would be unfair. It was not merely a military conquest. The institutions they created over four centuries of colonialism gave Britain a form of organisation which has held through to the present day.

Skill at road building and water engineering is the most quoted example, but coinage, taxation, the Latin language, and the extension of local government beyond village boundaries and the immediate family to provincial level, were Roman products of lasting benefit.

The Romans built the main road from Gloucester to Bath which came through Frocester and climbed the steep Cotswold escarpment zigzag fashion through Buckholt Wood to Coaley Peak. From here it went over Stonehill, which is the highest local point at around 800 feet above sea level, over the village cross roads, along Front Street, past the Street Farm and the present Post Office, down the Hollow Way and the Plain, up a stiffish climb at Townsend where generations of my own family, Smiths and Mills, were to raise their families, past Field Farm, and the head of the Kinley valley, to Kingscote and Lasborough and on to Bath whose Roman name was Aquae Sulis, the waters of the sun.

The crossroads in Nympsfield was the crossing of two equally important Roman roads; the Gloucester–Bath road was crossed by the east–west road from the provincial capital at Cirencester to the Roman garrison at Uley Bury.

Nailsworth did not exist in Roman times, and even in Domesday Book recorded in 1086, it gets no mention. Stroud is another town that grew up later as shown by its absence from the Domesday Book. When Nailsworth did develop it did so on the route of the old Roman road from Cirencester to Uley Bury, in the shelter of the valley bottom, and with the weight of water from a number of streams to provide power.

The straight road from Cirencester to Uley Bury would have gone through Minchinhampton where the Dobunni had their capital behind the impressive bulwarks at the start of the Roman push across southern England, down through what is now Nailsworth and up past Forest Green Rovers football ground to Nympsfield. I have measured it as being around fifteen miles. Through Cherington and Avening it is seventeen miles. Either way a good walk as my forebears Moses and Charles Smith were to discover.

Roman times were still hard times for the people. Deaths in childbirth, and amongst children were still very high; the average lifespan for men was thirty-six years and for women a mere twenty-eight years.

This brings me to my two final points about the Roman conquest. I mentioned that it was 'a good walk' and gave it in miles not kilometres. There has to be a further explanation because I was referring to English miles and not Roman miles. The English mile was 1760 yards which in metric language is just over 1609 metres: the Roman mile was 1617 yards or about 1479 metres.

Interestingly this is so close to the metric mile of 1500 metres that one wonders if the Roman influence throughout Europe for so many centuries had paved the way for the modern metric system of measurement, but research produced almost the opposite answer. It was Roman adoption of earlier Greek measuring units that produced the inch and the mile and persisted into the Middle Ages in Europe. It was the French who introduced the metric system in 1795 and through the Napoleonic Wars saw it accepted over most of mainland Europe.

The final point concerns the presence of Christians in the country from at least the beginning of the conquest in 43 AD.

The Seventh Legion stationed at Gloucester was honoured with the special title of the Claudian Legion, and was under the command of Aulus Plautius. He was a General reporting directly to the Emperor Claudius, and was a cousin of Claudius' first wife.

When Claudius left Britain after only a short stay to return to Rome he left Aulus Plautius as Propaetor or governor general of the country. The wife of Aulus Plautius was Pomponia Graecina who in 57 AD was accused of allegiance 'to a foreign superstition', of which charge she was acquitted but by a court in her favour, presided over by her husband Aulus Plautius.

It is likely that this 'foreign superstition' was Christianity and although early Christian traditions do not mention her as a Christian, nevertheless Tactitus wrote that she was, and Tindal in his 'Notes on Rapin's History of England' claimed that she was the first Christian in Britain, though other claims have been made for that title.

She had a close British woman friend, Claudia Ruffina, who later married Rufus Pudens and had a son Linus. It had been claimed that this was the Linus who became the second Bishop of Rome in 67, but although this is possible it is not certain.

Much of this is conjecture, but certainly these legends have persisted, and Nicholas Wiseman (1802–1865), on being raised in 1850 to be the first Cardinal resident in England since the Reformation, and Archbishop of Westminster, took the name Pudens, Claudia's husband, as his patron saint.

In St. Paul's Second Epistle to Timothy, Chapter 4 Verse 21 we read 'Eubulus greets you, and so do Pudens, Linus, Claudia, and all the brethren'. Surely these names are not just a coincidence? There was only a small minority of Christians in Rome at this time and it must be unlikely that another identical group would have been repeated amongst so few; the chronology is right as well. These were the close friends and supporters of Paul, and this was the epistle he wrote at the very end of his ministry when he was preparing for his death, yet he still found time to remember them.

A question may also be raised against the claim that Claudia was British but whereas Claudia is Roman, Ruffina is most certainly British, and may be traced through to the present-day Griffith. Just as the Roman Legion at Gloucester was given the special title of the Claudian Legion, and the city of Gloucester was first called Claudiocestriae, may it not have been possible that Claudia was an adopted name also?

It was centuries later that St. Augustine arrived in Kent under orders from Pope Gregory I and succeeded in converting London and the South East to Roman Church organisation and rule. That was in 597, the year that St. Columba died, the same Irish missionary who is credited with the conversion of Scotland.

Whatever may be the claims for St. Augustine, supporters of the early primitive church were over here from very early days.

The Earliest Christian Community at Nympsfield

Until recent years, the earliest Christian foundation was thought to be the pre-Conquest Anglo-Saxon priory dedicated to the Virgin Mary and a chantry chapel dedicated to St. Anthony, the father of monasticism, at Kinley Meadow on Upper Lutheridge Farm to the south of Nympsfield village.

With the remarkable discovery of a Roman temple on land opposite Hetty Pegler's Tump, this view has become outdated, for there is evidence that this pagan site dedicated to Mercury, was converted to a Christian church in the post-Roman fifth century as suggested by its east-west orientation.

Sadly both sites have been lost for excavation purposes, and we will have to work on present evidence.

The first reference to Kinley (Kyneley, or Kyngeley) is an annal of 862. A later reference dated 1429 reports 'the free chapel of Kyngeley in the parish of Nympsfield ... the foundaycion of such chapel can be by no means found or seen.' According to the Register of Chantries in 1542 soon after the dissolution of the monasteries 'there only remains of the priory a very small ruin, which is not worth notice'.

From these reports a monastic settlement existed at Kinley before 862 and had disappeared as a place of work and worship before 1429. To these slender facts we can add that although the royal Northumbrian line had converted to Christianity in 627, the Mercian King Penda was a pagan still at his death in 645. It is to Osric king of the Hwiccii, that the mass conversion of the people in this area can be attributed around 655. By 676 Osric had founded an abbey at Bath at the extreme south of his kingdom which was formed by the River Avon. In 679 Ostric had installed a Bishop at Worcester to cover his kingdom, and a new see was created to the west with its boundary along the River Leadon and its centre at Hereford. This was to remain until Henry VIII came to the throne (1509–1547) and created the diocese of Gloucester. In 681 Osric founded as a minster the Abbey of Gloucester, and appointed a woman, the Abbess Kyneburg whom some historians say was his sister, to be in charge.

Between 655 and 681 when Osric started his campaign of Christian building and organisation, the historic Synod of Whitby had taken place in 664 when the church in England took the important change in direction and adopted Roman usages and came under the rule of Rome. It was an era of revolutionary change.

In the wave of convertitis that ensued under Osric, over a dozen new religious houses were created and it must be a probability that Kinley was founded at that time in the late seventh century.

There is just one more fact to emphasise what some may consider pure hypothesis.

The Abbess Kyneburg was followed at Gloucester by two more women who ruled until about 767 when the abbey went into decline and until 817 lay desolate and in ruins. The abbey was then rebuilt and this was completed in 823 and until 1022 lay in the control of secular priests who were allowed to marry: so it is unlikely that Kinley would have been created after 767.

So let us look at this scenario. A Christian king with the ambition and determination to make his mark in life sets out with religious fervour to promote and develop the Christian church covering the same area as his kingdom. He is supported by his family, two of whom were to be canonized, such was their devotion. At the Roman centres of Gloucester and Bath he establishes minsters.

On the road from Gloucester to Bath he builds a church at Frocester which like the other two is dedicated to St. Peter. At the top of the Cotswold escarpment on this same old Roman road, he establishes a priory, and in true Antonian tradition he builds a chantry in the peace and calm of a desolate hilltop. The site has no name. Someone suggests the Kings ley, the meadow or open clearing in woodland. Perhaps Osric wishes to honour his 'sister', Kyneburg. The 1429 reference was after all to Kyngeley. Hypothesis perhaps but it would make sense if it could be proved.

Nothing now remains of Kinley. The Ordnance Survey Archaeological Division accepts Kinley meadow on Upper Lutheridge Farm as its probable site.

A Saxon font was found in the valley being used as a water trough, and an old piscina was also found in the area. They have been retrieved and are in use again in the R.C. Church at Nympsfield.

The need for water nearby is also well covered at Kinley for the coomb is steep and water tumbles down to a deep pond. It is called Kinley Roar. It falls over twenty-seven stones which would have aided aeration. It could have been used for washing and fulling home-made cloth. At the pool animals may well have found drinking water, but it may also have served as a washpool, as at Horsley further downstream, for the dipping and washing of sheep before shearing.

The choice of St. Anthony, to whom the chantry chapel was dedicated, was apt. St. Anthony lived a hermit's life and practised asceticism. He withdrew for absolute solitude to a mountain where he lived for about twenty years. His followers at Kinley would have found an ideal setting there to carry out his rule of life. Nor did this life style cause St. Anthony any great problems, for he lived more than one hundred years.

From Roman to Norman: The First Millennium

The post Roman-British period after the defeat of the rump of Roman troops under Constantine III in 411 was a defining point in time, but the gradual withdrawal of Roman soldiers had been taking place over much of the fourth century. The Roman army which had totalled 63,000 men at its peak was never to return. The administration slowly ground to a halt, and Britain reverted to the barbarism of local chieftains. There were sporadic attacks from outsiders from Ireland, Scotland, and from mainland Europe, led by the Angles and Saxons and finally the Danes and Norman French. It is a period covering six centuries, and deserves the description of the Dark Ages.

The arrival of the Saxon invaders climaxed in their victory in battle in 577 at Dyrham Park which is just north of the present M4 and near the Fosse Way.

What we now know as Gloucestershire was as important to the Anglo-Saxons as to the Romans. Their trade was dependent on coal and iron ore from the Forest of Dean, and coins were minted. There was a royal palace at Kingsholm which then stood outside the old Roman city of Gloucester.

King Athelstan one of our most powerful Kings who ruled over a larger part of England than any of his predecessors, died at Gloucester, and was buried at Malmesbury in 954. His successor Edmund was killed at Pucklechurch in 960 defending his bailiff from an armed robber.

Edward the Confessor who came to the throne in 1042 was

known not to have travelled north of Gloucester but regularly came to the city using the palace at Kingsholm as his base whilst hunting in the Forest of Dean. He held regular witans in Gloucester, and from this history's point of view, he married Edith the daughter of Earl Godwin(e) the most powerful man in England at the time, who was lord of the manor of Berkeley and who took over the manor of Woodchester: arguably the most important lord of the manor in all Nympsfield's history.

Earl Godwin's involvement with Nympsfield is yet another example of boundary changes by force and not agreement and the 'stolen fields theory' already presented. In this instance Earl Godwin gave the Woodchester manor to his wife the Countess Gytha.

> 'that she might be maintained from thence when he abode at Berkeley: for she was unwilling to eat anything from that manor (Berkeley) on account of the destruction of the abbey'.

This refers to the Berkeley minster which was of great importance in church history at the time as two of its Abbots had been promoted direct to become Bishop of Worcester.

In the Abingdon version of the Domesday Book.

> 'Godwin had a bad reputation as a robber of churches ... he did all too little penance for the property of God which he held belonging to many holy places'.

Here we have as lord of the Manor of Nympsfield, Earl Godwin, king-maker and breaker, and his wife Gytha, who were related by marriage to King Canute. Here too were the parents of Edith, wife and Queen consort of Edward the Confessor; and here were the parents of Harold who succeeded his father Godwin as the most powerful man in England prior to the arrival of the Normans, and who succeeded to the throne of England on the Confessor's death, but lost his life and throne to William the Conqueror at the Battle of Hastings in 1066.

Domesday Book also records that in 1086 Roger de Berkeley was Lord of the manor of neighbouring Dursley and he was a cousin of King Edward the Confessor.

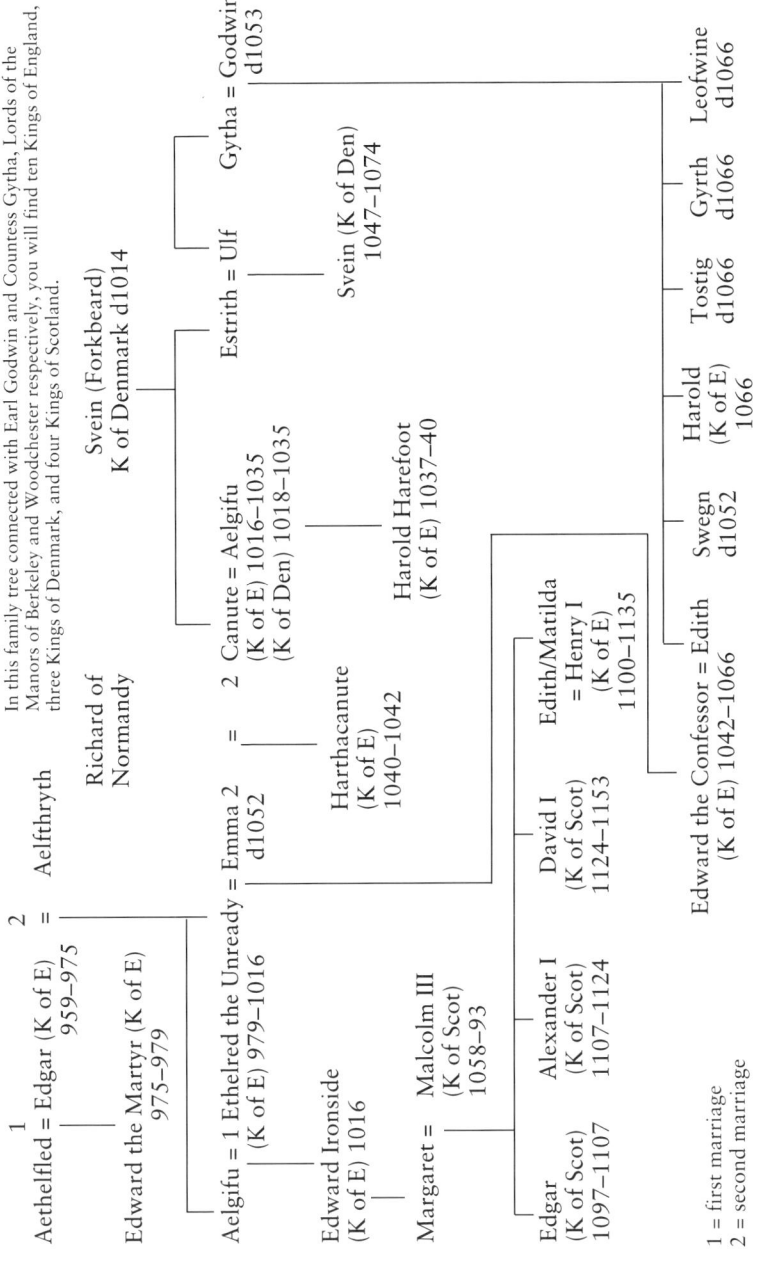

William the Conqueror held court at Gloucester at Christmas 1085 and continued the close connection with the city established by his Anglo Saxon predecessors. The witan lasted five days but it was arguably the most important parliament of his reign, for it was then decided to hold the Domesday Survey of England.

This was done with the specific purpose of establishing all the facts necessary to calculate how much tax could or should be extracted for the royal coffers, the churches, and finally for Rome. Gloucestershire was the most fertile farmland in the country and its revenues were well milked: it was not however a good time for its people. Most were serfs living a life of slavery and living in abject poverty. For them it was a life of toil from daybreak to sundown with no respite. Whilst William the Conqueror enriched himself and his soldiery, and then paid Rome in English silver, the peasantry who did the physical hard labour owned nothing, working ceaselessly to survive. When harvests failed or winters were very hard, they had no medicines to defend their bodies and no help to get better; they were left to die. Theirs was the story of the goose that laid the golden egg, for without their labour there was no crop.

The Normans were fine builders of churches and this has no doubt led them to be admired and respected, but they were ruthless and cruel, savage and ambitious and charged with power and the drive to pillage in the same way as their Viking predecessors. These were hard days for local people, probably the hardest in our long history. The change when William Rufus came to the throne on his father's death was negligible. To the above characterisation should be added untrustworthiness and disloyalty in the case of William II.

From Nympsfield's point of view the Norman period saw the creation of the Berkeley dynasty.

Robert Fitzharding, a Bristol merchant, gave support to Prince Henry the great grandson of William the Conqueror, and son of the arrogant Matilda the daughter of Henry I and the only legitimate child to out-live him. Henry I had been the father of at least twenty-two children, but only two legitimate, and his son and heir had died before him. Matilda's cousin Stephen had become King, and there followed nineteen years of anarchy which left England war-weary for change. Fitzharding chose well and in 1152 the Prince who was to become our first Plantagenet monarch granted him the manor of Berkeley and nine manors on the Cotswold escarpment including Wotton under Edge and Dursley, containing the village of Nympsfield: the Berkeley dynasty which has come down to the present day was founded.

Pre-Reformation Gloucestershire: The Seeds of Capitalism are Sown

With the end of the Norman period came the last time that this country had to suffer the pillage of foreign invaders, and we enter a new period in our history. Foreign influence was on the wane, and the separate powers of Crown and Church were to be the recipients of that lessening light. In 1215 King John signed the Magna Carta under pressure from his barons who were his own officer class. The Pope demanded that John should repudiate the Magna Carta, and the barons threatened to call in the French Dauphin, Louis. The dark clouds of foreign intervention again appeared on the horizon, and what must have seemed to many at the time as Divine intervention, took place when John unexpectedly died after what was described as a 'surfeit of peaches and new cider'. His ten year old son Henry, was crowned Henry III in great haste in the Abbey Church of Gloucester in the presence of his mother, Queen Isabella, and in the absence of a crown, her bracelet was placed upon his head.

A century later the manor of Berkeley was involved in another royal event, the distasteful and gruesome murder of Edward II in Berkeley Castle, and his burial in Gloucester. That was in 1327, and in 1331 work was commenced on the new cathedral.

Parliaments continued to be held on occasion in Gloucester:

by order of Edward I in 1279, Richard II in 1378, and Henry IV in 1407.

Royal families changed, and new dynasties were formed. New Popes and Bishops passed across the scene for better or for worse, and not always for the better. The invasion of foreign armies from mainland Europe had ended, and this part of our history was now to be reversed with the newly organised English taking advantage of the undeveloped nation across the Channel.

Our island geography was to enable and encourage us to develop our own language, literature, society, and industry without foreign intrusion, and with our own created wealth which for centuries had been plundered by Europe's soldiers and churchmen.

It is from the Middle Ages post Norman to the Tudor Reformation, covering four hundred years, that we see the sowing of the first seeds of capitalism and entrepreneurial skills. From now on it was the ability to produce and barter and deliver on time that built up England's strength and economic power.

It is a period in our history that saw the first moves towards religious change and reform, but we should remember that the decisive moves of Henry VIII in 1536–40 to abolish the monasteries could not have taken place if the Church had been popular and widely supported; it had lost its way, and was enjoying the wealth and power gained from its vast estates whilst poverty prevailed around it. It is a crude assessment to refer only to Henry VIII and his divorce of Catherine of Aragon as the cause of schism in the Catholic Church. Those who make that claim without any criticism of the modus operandi of the existing Church at the time are not facing the facts.

Henry Tudor's manoeuvre against the friars and monks and their institutions only succeeded because there was a great deal of unrest and criticism within the Church itself. Had there been a united and forward-looking Church against him, Henry VIII would have failed as surely as John before him at Runneymede.

What Henry achieved without intending it, was the privatisation of the means of production, which left his daughter

Elizabeth to develop the means of distribution with the merchant venturers.

As Professor Trevelyan put it in his History of England (1st Ed 1944)

> 'The crash of monastic masonry resounding through the land was ... a demolition order to resolve at one stroke a social problem that had been maturing for two centuries past.'

It was the end of mediaeval society in England: coincidentally it was the earliest point at which I can trace a member of my family in Nympsfield.

Through my grandmother Jane Mills there is a line back to John Mills who was elected Tithingman (a sort of Inland Revenue official) at a Court Leet in 1543 (Glos Notes & Queries V p 86 – Berkeley Hundred Court Rolls).

Henry VIII was not merely destructive in his religious reforms. At the surrender of St. Peter's Abbey he founded the diocese of Gloucester by taking it away from Worcester which had controlled it for at least 850 years, and handed it over to the care of the Dean and Chapter. Kings School which had existed since the twelfth century – it is mentioned in a charter of 1199 – was made an integral part of Gloucester Cathedral and the Dean and Chapter became its governors. In 1540 Crypt Grammar School was founded, and Bristol Cathedral School was created in 1542.

For the ordinary working man – the serfs, villeins, or feudal tenants who were not allowed to leave their land and were entrapped within their manors – one event stood out in this post Norman pre-Reformation epoch; the Black Death of 1348–9. It had a lasting effect in favour of those who lived.

The population was cut perhaps by half, and as disease was unimpressed by rank or fortune, the style of farming had to change drastically. The religious order at Kinley with its priory and chantry became vacant and even eight years after the plague had passed Kinley remained untilled by 1356. For the landlord who lived, there was a greatly reduced labour force at his disposal, and the land under plough had likewise to be reduced: he turned from arable to grass. The farming of sheep took over, giving England the chance with the ensuing surplus of wool to sell more overseas, and eventually to turn to home-made cloth and a secondary cottage industry. Here was work for the womenfolk and the entry into our language of the word spinster. It was the working man and woman's opportunity and they took it.

At the same time it gave England the development of the yeoman and the birth of the middle class; the wide gap between lord of the manor, or squire and the peasant was being narrowed and filled.

The Old Families of Nympsfield

Reference has already been made to John Mills in 1543 as an elected officer of the Berkeley Hundred dealing with Nympsfield.

Later in that century in 1584 half way through Elizabeth's long reign, the land accounts of Nympsfield mention John Pegler, Jeffrey Paine, Thomas Hoskins, and William Cowley, and refer to a number of strips of land owned by Richard Smith who is the earliest of the Smith family on the male line that I have discovered.

In 1608 in John Smyth's Register of Men and Arms in Gloucestershire which listed all those in every manor in the county who owned arms or had a horse that could be ridden, there are four Smiths; the afore mentioned Richard Smith who is described as 'being unable in body' but in possession of a calyver or short gun; William Smith who was near the top of the list being a yeoman farmer, followed by Pearse Smith and Tobye Smith who were broad cloth weavers being involved in the growing and considerable cloth trade carried on as a cottage industry and which provided the best income from any occupation at the time and for many years to come.

In 1725 the parish records show the death of Mary Smith, widow of Jeremiah. Surprisingly this entry is not out of chronological order, as she is said to have died aged 107 years, and that puts her birth at 1618.

Out of twenty-six men listed, four were Smiths, and four

were Peglers. The four Peglers were skilled craftsmen; one carpenter and three weavers. There was no clothier in Nympsfield but neighbouring Uley had three such middlemen who would merchant and transport the finished article.

The question might well be asked why should it have been thought necessary in 1608 to make such an inventory? Only three years earlier in 1605 just two years into the reign of James I, the first of the Scottish Stuart Kings, there had been the attempt to blow up Parliament in the name of Guy Fawkes and the ensuing fragile peace was still on red alert.

The year 1678 records the birth of Piers Smith, and in 1679 the marriage of Susannah Bushell, a forebear of my great grandmother Mary Ann Bushell, is to be found. Charles II was still on the throne of England, and Louis XIV on the throne of France.

Harriet is a frequently recurring forename in the Smith family, and in 1681 Harriet, daughter of Robert Smith, married Cornelius, son of Thomas Sparks. In 1684, John Mills married Sarah Adey from Rodborough, and two baptisms were those of Judith, daughter of William and Mary Burford, and Dorothy, daughter of George and Mary Pegler. There were further baptisms in 1686 starting with James son of John and Mary Smith; Catharine daughter of John and Mary Burford; Hannah daughter of Abel and Hannah Bushell; Margaret daughter of William and Elizabeth Burford; William and Hannah the children of Thomas and Abigail Mills; and finally a son – the writing is illegible – to Thomas and Mary Burford.

It will be noticed even from this small cross-section of the records from 1684 how often the forename Mary is used. My great grandfather Moses married twice and both times to a Mary Ann; and his mother was also a Mary. Nowadays it is widely used in the Catholic Church but not often in the Anglican Church. To emphasise this, in 1682 William Ridler who was an Anabaptist had his daughter's birth recorded, and the entry made said 'the name of Mary was imposed'. If this implies an attitude of 'take it or leave it' from the Church of England then we should not be surprised, for to this time is dated the story of the mounds, now levelled but still clearly visible as having been burial sites just inside the graveyard near the small gate at the bottom east entrance. These are said to be the graves of local Quakers who buried their dead at night; as the parish records have it, without any hint of charity – 'without Christian burial'. They were hard-hearted times indeed. How difficult it must have been to have held religious views that differed from the Established Church or the lord of the manor. A century and a half later the coin was to turn again.

In the sixteenth century reference has been made to the family names of Mills, Pegler, Paine, Hoskins, Cowley and Smith; when the parish records began in the late seventeenth century thirty families appeared in the first decade. In alphabetical order they are Adey, Baker, Brown, Burford, Bushell, Cole, Dangerfield, Davis, Estcort, Hammond, Heskins, Hill, Hinton, Hodges, Howell, Kedwelly, Knight, Lewis, Mills, Parsons, Payne (or Paine), Pearse, Pegler, Shillam, Siseham, Smith, Sparks, Taylor, Turtle, and Wayte (or Weight).

From the earliest days of parish records back to the first half of the sixteenth century, there are two families, Mills and Pegler, that have come through without break to the present day, well over four hundred years.

The Smith family gets its earliest mention in the land accounts of 1584 along with the Pegler family, but that particular line ended at Nympsfield with the burial of my grandfather Charles Smith's eldest sister, my great aunt Harriet Pegler who died in 1913; a continuous line of at least 329 years, but which without doubt was much farther back in time, as were the other old families. In the Mills family connection with Nympsfield, the earliest date of 1543 takes us back over four hundred and fifty years.

There are nine families that occur regularly throughout most of those years although they are not all in the present village; Burford, Bushell, Daniels, Gingell (from 1730), Mills, Neale, Pegler, Smith, Witchell (from 1745).

Writing the history of a village and its surrounding district based on your own family and its connections runs at some stage into outside criticism that it is too subjective. This is the stage now reached when that statement becomes an apology, for in referring to the old families of Nympsfield the c19 produced four families that moved away and made a name for themselves. In so doing it is hoped that readers will find this brief record of interest.

In alphabetical order the families are Daniels, King, Smith and Townsend.

In 1840 the first Daniels to leave were blacksmiths and millwrights. They moved to Lightpill where they set up a pattern-making and machine shop and started making machinery for the corn milling and textile industries. As they developed they moved into gas producing plant and oil engines with their own patented brand name of Trusty, the forerunners of diesel engines used in mining and on railways. Daniels of Lightpill produced the first steam and oil engines for ships' propellers. The name T.H. & J. Daniels has now gone but their successors have continued on the same site with pumps and presses for the plastics industry.

From the same family came Francis Daniels who married Charlotte, the youngest daughter of Moses Smith. Francis left Nympsfield to become headmaster of the British School at Ebley. He later became an insurance agent, and in 1891 was appointed Midlands manager of the Sceptre Life Association. In 1893 he formed the Birmingham Mutual Sick Benefit and Old Age Society that changed its name to the Ideal Benefit Society in 1906. In 1896 he founded the Birmingham Mutual Bank that changed its name to the Ideal Bank in 1914; the bank was taken over by Barclays Bank in 1957. In 1932 the Ideal Assurance Co. Ltd was formed out of the Benefit Society, and in the following year Francis William Daniels died. A Birmingham City Councillor and magistrate he had created the 'Ideal way of life'.

Perhaps the respect in which he was held was best shown by his being called to give evidence in 1907 to the Royal Commission on the Poor Law, and in 1911, after the last Liberal Government passed the first National Health Insurance Act, he was invited to join the Advisory Committee to the Commissioners.

The other three families have their connections with the agricultural ancillary trades.

The Townsend family farmed Court Farm, and it was one of their family named Richard who founded the business of R. Townsend & Co. Ltd at Stratford Mill, Stroud, which is now the site of Tesco supermarket. It was bought first by Rank

Hovis McDougal who later sold to Dalgety Agriculture; was nationally known for its seeds and seed corn.

Reference has already been made to Professor John King. He was born in 1927 the only son of John Victor Beaufoy King and was baptised at St. Bartholomew's, Nympsfield. His uncle farmed Tinkley Farm whilst his father ran Egypt Mill in Nailsworth started by John King's grandfather. The company was named J.B. King & Sons and was succeeded by another miller named King but no relation to the Nympsfield Kings. Egypt Mill is now a thriving hotel and restaurant complex run by Stephen Webb who married John King's cousin. One of Professor King's sons was a member of the team of scientists who produced Dolly the cloned sheep.

Some time after 1851 my great grandfather Moses, by then in his thirties and with five children, of whom only the last two had survived, decided to look elsewhere for employment and became a pork butcher with Cole & Lewis in Cirencester. This entailed a weekly walk from Nympsfield of fifteen miles, taking lodgings at Cirencester and returning at the weekend. When old enough he took his eldest living son, Charles, with him to learn the trade. Moses then decided to set up on his own and so the business of Moses Smith and Son was started.

When Moses died in 1895 Charles continued on his own, and in 1906 formed the bacon curing company of Smith Rogers & Co. Ltd. at Ebley. Then began one of the earliest attempts at vertical integration. Rogers appears to have got cold feet and withdrew, but Charles Smith, by now well established, had financial support from Walter Bingham who was chairman of the Ocean Accident & Guarantee Corporation. His scheme was to produce everything in production from start to finish.

He took over two three hundred acre farms, Bown Hill above Woodchester and Park Farm in the Severn Valley at Cambridge, to grow barley and rear a commercial herd of Wessex Saddleback pigs; he bought the corn merchant business W. Knight & Co at Ebley Oil Mill to convert the barley into pig food; he purchased a quarter of a mile of pig sties behind the Kings Head at Eastington for the fattening pigs; he set up a string of retail shops for direct sale of finished products; he established a wholesale business and a contract to distribute throughout Wales with the Melias chain of shops.

It failed at the beginning of the Great War because of its success: demand had outstripped production and he had to buy in pigs and in doing so bought in swine fever in one year and erysipelas in the next.

Disease in two successive years stopped a bold enterprise and the separate parts of the business operated independently from then on. The bacon curing firm was sold eventually to Matthesons who sold on to Walls, the assets stripped and the property sold off. Joe Norris who married my cousin Kathleen Smith farmed Bown Hill Farm until 1935 when he sold it to Cecil Lister of R.A. Lister of Dursley, and Smiths Superfeed Ltd of Ebley Oil (Corn) Mill ceased production in 1994, selling the property to David Guinness of the Guinness banking and investment arm.

A Story from the Civil War

Every war produces its heroes and anti-heroes, and Edward Massey, who began the Civil War on the side of King Charles I, switched his allegiance to the Parliamentarians under Oliver Cromwell, and finally reverted to support for the Crown, is one man who qualifies under both descriptions.

Massey was a professional soldier and ambitious; furthermore he was competent and fully convinced of his own abilities. It was his failure to convince the King of his abilities and the King's meanness and refusal to promote Massey that led the professional soldier to reveal his mercenary nature and join Cromwell. He became a brilliant leader of the Parliamentary forces in the West of England and especially in the Siege of Gloucester in 1643 in what turned out to be the turning point of the Civil War.

Gloucester was the key strategic city in the Civil War because it was in 1643 the only urban area between Bristol and Worcester in Parliament's hands. Not for the first time in its history Gloucester owed its importance to its geographical position at the lowest fordable crossing point on the River Severn on its long route to the sea. Massey organised and led the successful defence of the city, and it is probable that had he not done so England's history from that point forward would have been a very different story.

From the viewpoint of this particular history, Massey's ability to escape custody and outwit his opponents, gives us a story that is not only worthy of being recounted but would make a great cinema or television scene.

In 1659, after Oliver Cromwell's death, the republic was in disarray and Massey had by now changed sides again and was working for the restoration of the monarchy. His ambitions to gain preferment had been rewarded with the rank of Major General.

The republican forces in Gloucester had heard news that Massey was to be found at Symonds Hall near Wotton under Edge under the roof of his relation, a Mr. Veal. Here he was discovered and seized by some troopers and along with his servant and Lord Herbert, a relation of the Duke of Beaufort, they were taken on horseback to Gloucester. Massey was put astride a trooper's horse sitting in front of his captor. The road they took was naturally the old Roman road from Bath to Gloucester that passed through Nympsfield.

The weather was bad, drenching rain and gale force winds, and at Buckholt Wood near the present Coaley Peak Picnic Site where the narrow road zigzagged down the steep escarpment to Frocester, Massey took the opportunity to unseat himself and his captor as the horse stumbled in the dark. In the commotion that followed Massey escaped into the wood and was not recaptured. His servant and Lord Herbert, who had been responsible back in March 1643 of raising an army of Welshmen to fight at Gloucester against Massey, were taken back to Gloucester alone.

Those who veer off the Cotswold Way on approaching Buckholt Wood will readily perceive that escape at that point would have been Massey's best bet, and Massey laid his bet well.

He was clearly an extraordinary man, and one of the outstanding personalities thrown up in this remarkable period in our history. The people of Gloucester revered him in spite of his changing sides more than once, and they twice elected him their M.P., first in 1646 and later in 1660. When Charles II was restored as King he made Massey a knight: Sir Edward Massey, the General who had four times escaped from captivity, twice from the Tower of London and once on the outskirts of Nympsfield at Frocester Hill.

St. Bartholomew's Church and the older buildings of Nympsfield

The Anglican Church stands on a site dating back to Saxon times; a chapel-at-ease to St. Peter's Church, Frocester. It is the oldest building in the village. The earliest part still standing is the late fifteenth century Perpendicular tower with a flat roof and battlements from which there is a pleasant view of the village. Like many Cotswold villages and towns – Cirencester is a good example – Nympsfield is built in a depression below the highest land point for reasons of shelter. The view therefore from the church tower is limited.

It carries a weathervane in the shape of a cockerel, and being cast in metal it reveals signs of having been used for target practice: some say by our American cousins whilst stationed in Woodchester Park during World War II.

The churchyard contains a number of yew trees which were planted intentionally and carried on a long tradition in English churches the reason for which seems to have been forgotten. The simple explanation is that the yew is poisonous to animals, so no matter how lush the grass was within the churchyard walls, the stockman made sure his cattle kept outside. In this way the sanctity and clean appearance of the burial ground was preserved.

Between 1861 and 1863 the main building was rebuilt to the designs of S.S. Teulon who did much work in the area around

Bust of Mercury, a copy of the original in British Museum.
By kind permission of Major Goldingham, taken in his house.

Long Barrow at Coaley Peak Picnic Site

St. Bartholomew's Church pre 1861, before the alterations by S.S. Teulon
(By kind permission of Ian Beales)

St. Bartholomew's Church after the alterations by S.S. Teulon between 1861 and 1864; taken from north east of church in morning sun.

St. Bartholomew's Church from the north showing the lych gate (right) and bench seat in the Garden of Remembrance (left)

Court Farm and St. Bartholomew's Church from Cockadilly showing the village in shallow combe for shelter

Drawing of the Dominican Priory Church of Our Lady of the Annunciation, Woodchester, by the author's son, Peter Smith.

St. Giles Church, Uley. Rebuilt by S.S. Teulon 1857–8

Marist Convent and Chapel built c1850, with additions around 1930

Chapel House (formerly the Red Lion) at Nympsfield Cross. Built in the Eighteenth century it is where the Dominicans first held Mass in the village. The War Memorial is in the shadow of house on the left

The Seventeenth century Rose & Crown Inn (formerly the Ducie Arms)

Bell Court, near the Four Wells (formerly the Bell Inn). King James II had a meal here in 1687 on a journey from Bath to Gloucester

Woodchester Park Mansion

John Evans, a Park Mansion guide, with David Armstrong of The National Trust inspect the sluice to old Park Mill at the bottom of the lowest lake of the five

Bown Hill Farm from near the Amberley Inn

Rose Westwood, Chair of Nympsfield Parish Council, and Ann Overton, who led the village to win the Britain in Bloom Heart of England village section in 1997 and 1998

this time: the churches at Uley, Newington Bagpath, Kingscote, and St. Mary's Woodchester, and arguably his most famous design, the monument at North Nibley to the honour of William Tyndale 'who first caused the New Testament to be printed in the mother tongue of his countrymen'. Teulon's monument to Tyndale reminds us that before the Reformation the Church had refused to allow the Holy Bible to be translated into English or any language but Latin.

The dedication of the Church first to St. Margaret and then to St. Bartholomew raises a number of questions. Which dedication is correct? Why was it changed? When was it changed?

The Rev. James Silvester in his 'History of Nympsfield Church' supports the choice of St. Bartholomew on the grounds that 'St. Bartholomew's Day is August 24th, and Nympsfield Feast falls about that day' but that seems an odd decision for a Christian church unless Nympsfield Feast was already celebrating a Christian ceremony. If it was not, then the change looks like a marriage of convenience.

A will dated 1508 refers to St. Margaret's Church and clearly it was so dedicated at that stage. Two more questions must now be asked. Did it change at the Reformation? Did it change after the Massacre of St. Bartholomew's Day in 1572?

Many Huguenots escaped from France after the latter event when over three thousand of their Protestant compatriots were killed in Paris alone. Pope Gregory XIII even went so far as to have a medal struck to commemorate it. We do know that many of these Huguenots came to this part of England, especially those with skills in the manufacturing trades of cloth and glass, and their family names still live on in the district; Clutterbuck and Malpass for example.

It seems to me that the more acceptable reason is that with the complete reorganisation of the Church of England at the time of the Reformation, the opportunity was given to adopt the new dedication to St. Bartholomew who was a popular figure in these parts. The earliest local dedication is to the Priory Hospital in Gloucester which was founded by Henry III in Lower Westgate Street. The oldest church dedication is to the village church at Aldsworth dating back to 1151. Since then there have been seven other churches so dedicated: Cam, Newington Bagpath, Notgrove, Nympsfield, Oakridge,

Whittington, and Winstone. There is only one dedication to St. Margaret and that is at Bagendon.

The popularity of St. Bartholomew in rural parishes can be partly explained because he was the patron saint of tanners one of the basic essential country trades.

The first Bartholomew to be canonised came from Armenia and was one of the twelve apostles. He had another personal name, Nathanael (John 1:43–51) and as 'bar' means 'son of' his full title would have been Nathanael, son of Tolomew, or Tolmai.

As for the rejected Margaret she was from Antioch and also a martyr; like Bartholomew she too had another name which in her case was Marina. She came from the third or fourth century and her feast day was July 20th. St. Margaret was eliminated in the revised calendar of the Roman Catholic Church in 1969 because it is doubted whether she ever existed. Nevertheless she was a well loved saint in the Middle Ages and her voice was one of the three voices Joan of Arc claimed to have heard before battle at Orleans in 1429.

It is Professor Owen Chadwick's view that the change from St. Margaret to St. Bartholomew was more likely due to the common Reformation change of a dedication from a non-scriptural to a scriptural and apostolic one, and interestingly he added 'but St. Margaret was so important to childbirth she often remained'.

When King James II, England's last Roman Catholic monarch (1685–88), travelled from Bath to Gloucester on August 22nd, 1687 he arrived at Nympsfield for a change of horses and a meal at Bell Court, which was then one of the village's five public houses, and discovered everywhere a great commotion preparing for the Annual Feast. Whether this was the Nympsfield Feast or the Feast of St. Bartholomew's Day is not clear but the dates are close enough for convenience, and it would suggest that celebrating both events at the same time would have been a reasonable solution for everyone.

In 1985 the celebration of eight hundred years of both church and village life was made on St. Bartholomew's Day and actors from the BBC Radio programme, The Archers, took over the village and made it Ambridge for the day, so the feasting still goes on though nowadays for special years only.

Next to the Church is Court Farm which was built around 1600 – there is a doorway dated 1617. This has a tithe barn and would have been the administrative centre for the village in the middle ages as its title implies. In Front Street, on the old Roman road and opposite the Post Office, is Street Farm and a doorway here is dated 1613. These buildings are not at present in farm use and appear to be in need of some repair. Further down Front Street on the Plain is the house to which James II came in 1687 named Bell Court, which is seventeenth century and in which a seventeenth-century fireplace remains in the living room which also has a fine modelled ceiling in plaster.

The old Church of England village school which was built in great haste in 1846 when William Leigh bought the estate from the Earl of Ducie and gave the original school notice to quit their former school premises, is now the Village Hall, and is well used and quite adequate for the new purposes. This building is in Back Street and its adjoining property, the School House, was built in 1865 after the rebuild of St. Bartholomew's Church, by the same architect S. S. Teulon.

The only existing public house is the Rose & Crown at the junction of Front and Back Streets. It bustles with activity and is a popular eating and meeting place; highly recommended. It dates from the same period as Bell Court, and was once called the Ducie Arms in deference to the then lord of the manor. Uniquely it has a spring rising in the back of the building and the stream flows through the cellar where it cools the victuals and provides clear spring water for the house. In cloth making days it would have been used for cleansing the wool as well as the cloth and further reference to this will be made later.

All in all a busy place.

The Revival of Roman Catholicism

The arrival of William Leigh (1802–1873) who bought Woodchester Park estate in November 1845 from the second Earl Ducie, brought about the return of Roman Catholicism.
Leigh had been an Anglican at the High Church end of the religious spectrum. Educated at Eton and Brasenose College, Oxford, he had retained close touch with his old university, although he had never taken a degree, and was attracted to the Oxford Movement. Here Leigh met John Henry Newman, Edward Pusey, the Froude brothers, R.H. and J.A. and John Keble, brother of Thomas Keble, the rector of Bisley. It was Keble in fact, whose powerful sermon on national apostasy in 1833 had set the movement alight. The group was fired by fears that the Reform Act of 1832 which had made the first faltering steps along the road to universal suffrage and democracy, would lead to increasing subordination of the established church to parliamentary will.

The Oxford Movement also added strength to the Gothic revival in church architecture, and here was associated with Augustus Pugin who wrote a book entitled 'Contrasts' in 1843, in which he argued that there was a direct link between quality and character of society, and the calibre of its architecture; and that ideal was the Gothic style. It was to Pugin, who had become a convert to the Roman church in 1835, that Leigh went for advice on how to develop the Park.

Leigh became a Roman Catholic in March 1844. He was

living at the time at Little Aston Hall in Staffordshire where close neighbours were some Passionist Fathers, whose full title was the Congregation of the Discalced Clerks of the Most Holy Cross and Passion of our Lord Jesus Christ. Their leader was Father (later Blessed) Dominic Barberi (1792–1849) who was clearly a remarkable man. It was Barberi who had received Newman into the Roman Catholic Church in 1845, and it is inconceivable that Barberi was not involved in the conversion of Leigh also, living as they did in the same Staffordshire village.

Father Dominic Barberi was a man of no formal education, from a very poor background in his native Italy, and yet here he was in England capable of persuading men of the intellect of Newman and the wealth of Leigh to join the Roman church, and doing it as an itinerant priest speaking in a foreign tongue. He died at the young age of fifty-seven years, and it was sixty-two years later in 1911 that he was declared Venerable, and a further fifty two years later in 1963 that he was beatified as Blessed. Many members of his church locally are hopeful that he will one day be canonized.

As soon as he had joined the Roman Catholic church Leigh resolved that he would devote his life to their cause. He was a man whose enthusiasm knew no bounds, and if ever the saying 'generous to a fault' fitted anyone, it fitted William Leigh.

He had already promised £4,000 – a great deal of money in those days – towards the cost of the new Anglican Cathedral of St. Peter and St. Paul in Adelaide, South Australia, but this was cancelled when he joined the Roman Catholics. He began to use his considerable fortune on proselytising near his home in Staffordshire, but his zeal made him unpopular to the extent that he decided to remove elsewhere.

Never one to seek second-rate advice, Leigh contacted Bishop Nicholas Wiseman whom he had met through Wiseman's links with the leaders of the Oxford Movement. This was the man whom Pope Pius IX called to Rome in 1850 and made the first Cardinal resident in England since the Reformation, and Archbishop of Westminster.

Wiseman recommended Leigh to buy Woodchester Park and to take Father Dominic Barberi and the Passionists with him, and there establish a Catholic community at the centre of an area one hundred miles in circumference where the practice of Roman Catholicism had disappeared.

Earl Ducie had first put Woodchester Park on the market in 1843, and an advertising poster shows that 4000 acres were on offer including the whole of Nympsfield.

Of particular interest, in view of what happened, is the wording on the advertisement stating that on offer was

> 'The entire village of Nympsfield wherein are sixty one houses and the Ducie Arms (later the Rose & Crown) with political influence extending over Twelve hundred honest Yeomen'.

This was just eleven years after the first great Reform Act of 1832 yet here we have 'political influence' as a main selling point, reflecting the way people thought at the time about the power of the squire: –

> 'Here's to the squire and his relations,
> Who keep us in our proper stations.'

Remember too that the Catholic Emancipation Act had only been passed in 1829, a further three years back; and that you had to be an Anglican to be admitted to the university of Oxford before 1854; and that Nonconformists were equally barred with Roman Catholics. In November 1845, Woodchester and Nympsfield had a Roman Catholic as Lord of the Manor, and one who had publicly declared his intention to build a Catholic community on his estate where none had existed before.

Things would never be quite the same again.

Having brought the Passionists from Staffordshire, William Leigh bought Northfields House in Forest Green where they could live, and which they could use as a base for their spiritual work. He gave notice to the Church of England to quit his newly acquired property at the Cross in Nympsfield where the Anglicans had a village school, and some time later this house was used for the Catholic Mass, a Mission having been established by the Passionists in 1847 (see photograph).

At the same time he appointed Charles Hansom the architect for his religious buildings at Woodchester, a man far more suited to his financial means than Augustus Pugin, but who nevertheless was an architect of considerable talent and love of the Gothic revivalist style, as the existing Church of Our Lady of the Annunciation, and those who remember the original monastery demolished in 1971 will bear witness.

If the name Hansom rings a bell, it is probably because of the Hansom cab, that highly successful and popular means of transport designed by Charles Hansom's brother Joseph, and patented in 1836.

Work on the monastery began in 1846 and was completed in 1849. Sadly in that year Father Dominic Barberi died suddenly on Reading Station – the railway to Stroud had been opened four years earlier – and within a year Leigh had replaced the Passionists at Woodchester with the Dominicans, and the Black Friars were to remain until even after their monastery was pulled down in 1971.

Although Leigh concentrated his building programme on Woodchester, it did not stop him making his mark on Nympsfield right from the start. In 1851, the year both of my grandparents, Charles Smith and Jane Mills were born at Nympsfield, Robert Burford, the Parish Overseer, whose duties included the administration of poor relief, recorded 'the year was a very troublesome time for me and all the parish'. William Leigh had ordered good houses to be pulled down and had 'covered up good wells, the best in the parish for water' which could hardly have endeared him to the villagers.

That Leigh pursued a policy of proselytism as he had done at Little Aston can hardly be doubted. His zeal as a convert was natural to him; moreover, like Newman he felt he had a point to make, and a point to prove. In neither case did it bring popularity. Leigh suffered also from the misfortune of bad timing.

When Leigh came to the district in November 1845 the Roman Catholic Church was growing rapidly in England, partly because of conversions, but also because of the three devastating years of potato crop failure in Ireland starting in 1845 which saw a large influx of Irish labourers escaping the ravages of famine. Fortunately for them the head of the

Catholics in England was Bishop Wiseman who, as the son of a farmer from Co. Waterford, was well placed to receive them with sympathy and care. On the other hand they also provided extra competition for jobs and an excuse for employers to hold down wages.

A newly-elected Pope, Pius IX came into office in 1846 and met resistance from the Papal States who were agitating for a unified Italy. With revolutions spreading in Europe, Pius IX fled from Rome to Naples in 1848, but in 1850, back in Rome, he decided to restore the English Hierarchy and appointed Bishop Wiseman as Cardinal Archbishop of Westminster.

There was outrage throughout England on what was felt to be an assault on the established Church: three centuries had passed since the Reformation. On November 5th 1850 the effigy of Guy Fawkes was replaced throughout England by effigies of the Pope and Cardinal Wiseman, such was their unpopularity: not a good time for a new landlord to attempt mass conversion of his tenants to the Catholic faith.

On top of all this Leigh appears to have met opposition from two sections of the community that were poles apart.

First from those over whom he had purchased 'political influence'. They had lost the leadership of a family who had been their lords of the manor for two hundred years. Earl Ducie had been M.P. for East Gloucestershire as a Whig, and now sat in the House of Lords, and his father had been Lord Lieutenant of Gloucestershire. It was an old county family which had once been bankers to the Royal family. In its place had come an outsider from Staffordshire whose family business interests had been in shipping, and especially on the government's behalf in the deportation of convicts to Australia, and then on the return journey calling on ports in Africa and taking part in the slave trade. All of which was perfectly legal before 1807 and most certainly profitable, but left doubts and question marks.

Secondly from those at the head of the Roman Catholic Church, there was the hesitancy and caution over all converts, and in Leigh's case, in spite of his education at Eton and Oxford, he represented new money and trade.

This probably accounts for the scarcity of information on William Leigh, and that despite his important contacts and undoubted generosity, he never appears as one who was fully accepted at any level of society.

Today time the great healer has witnessed the turmoil of the mid-nineteenth century turn to comparative tranquillity, and Nympsfield appears at peace with itself. The spirit of ecumenism now exists where even in recent years there was none at all, and for that the clergy on both sides of the religious divide can take credit. Liturgical differences still exist, and there would be no point in two churches pursuing a separate course if there were none, but at least those differences can be understood and respected without cries of heresy, and unity can exist without union.

Woodchester Park

This is a chapter that justifies a book on its own. In spite of its name it is inextricably linked with Nympsfield.

Until well into this century the lord of the manor of Nympsfield, Woodchester, Frocester, and Kingstanley was the head of the Leigh family, and it was William Leigh who took over Woodchester Park from the Earl of Ducie in 1845. Before that in the reign of Elizabeth the First it was the manorial seat of the Huntley family who were at Frocester Court when the Queen stayed overnight en route for Berkeley Castle in 1574.

The Huntley seat in Woodchester was the house now called the Old Priory owned by Captain A.H. Villiers and earlier by the Metcalfe family. The Old Priory was rebuilt in 1512 on a very early site which is part of the famous Roman pavement. It was never a priory in the sense of a religious building but could have been connected with the previous Christian church which sadly did so much damage by using the old Roman site as its burial ground.

George Huntley, who was later knighted, became lord of the manor in 1580, and was the man who rode roughshod over commoners rights at the top end of the valley by creating Spring Park and enclosing much common land behind a stone wall. It was he who built a hunting lodge on the site where the unfinished mansion now stands.

In 1631 the Woodchester estate was sold to Sir Robert Ducie, and so began a series of events involving two families, the Ducies and the Leighs, and the influence of a priest, Fr

Dominic Barberi, all of whom were connected by domicile with Little Aston in Staffordshire.

Huntley's Lodge was converted into a permanent residence some time after 1613, possibly during the Civil War (c 1643) but certainly well before 1750 when Frederick Prince of Wales, the heir to George II, stayed at the house then called Spring Park. It was at this time that the Prince told Matthew Ducie Moreton, the first Lord Ducie that he ought to have a decent pair of gates at the entrance to his property and these were made by Edward Smith of Nympsfield and placed at the entrance by Coaley Peak. They were built at a forge on the Cross where Smith had been apprenticed to Benjamin Mills, and had married his daughter Rachel.

In 1782 Capability Brown visited the Park but he was in the last year of his life, and it was his assistant, John Spyer, who formally surveyed the estate. In 1783 the redesign of the fishponds was begun which over the years has made the present series of five lakes, set against a backdrop of mature woodlands, into an unrivalled scene of pastoral beauty.

It should be added that Lord Ducie also took advice from Humphrey Repton in 1809, for a quarter of a century had passed since the visit of Capability Brown and the survey by Spyers. There can be no doubt that this masterpiece of landscaping is the brainchild of the two outstanding designers of the c18 and c19 Britain. For me it transcends the Gothic intricacy and skilled stonemasonry of the unfinished Woodchester Park Mansion.

Lancelot 'Capability' Brown (1715–83) has left his trade mark in the natural, easy, and unforced appearance of still freshwater lakes and sweeping bands and clumps of trees. Humphrey Repton (1752–1818) his successor added to this plan by adopting a thicker tree planting scheme giving dense woodland right down to the water's edge, and this, his trade mark, coming second in time is the easier to follow.

The park land was the prime inspiration for the Ducie family; the building of the Gothic mansion was the driving force behind William Leigh. Together they have left to posterity something which is quite unique, and in these days of toil and trouble, rush and noise, Woodchester Park is a tranquil, restful, unspoilt bit of old English countryside at its best.

Today it is in the hands of the National Trust and a small management team led by David Armstrong.

The mansion, which has a Grade 1 listing, is owned by the Stroud District Council, and Woodchester Mansion Trust, a charity begun in 1989 by a local group, leases the building from them: with the support of English Heritage and the hardworking efforts of local volunteers centred on Nympsfield and in particular on the Post Office and the Chair of the Parish Council, Rose Westwood, the mansion is opened every first weekend in the months from April to October, and at Bank Holidays.

It would be a serious error if mention was not made of the late Reg Kelly. Long before the Trust was formed it was his efforts almost alone that saved the building from being vandalised and stripped. His wife was Chair of the Breakheart Hill Nature Reserve, and his daughter Ann Hardy grazes the fields opposite the mansion with Welsh Blacks, and a few cattle with a thick white band around the middle which is a rare and very old breed, the Belted Welsh Black. The sheep are Black Mountain Welsh, another rare breed.

Just as the Earl of Ducie had brought in the leading landscape gardeners to advise on the layout of the Park, so William Leigh brought in one of the leading architects in the country to design his mansion.

He chose Augustus Pugin, a London architect who was also a convert to Roman Catholicism, having joined in 1835. Amongst Pugin's works are Balliol College, Oxford, and extensive repairs and alterations to Alton Towers in Staffordshire. In his declining years he assisted Sir Charles Barry on the new Palace of Westminster.

Pugin did not come cheap, and his extravagant Gothic designs were not suited to Leigh's pocket, so Leigh then invited Charles Hansom, who had already designed the religious houses for Leigh in Woodchester. Finally he called in Benjamin Bucknall, a young local man born in Rodborough.

Bucknall was a follower and student of Eugene-Emmanuel Viollet-le-Duc (1814–79) the French Gothic Revival architect, famous for his restoration of Notre Dame in Paris in 1845, and of the Abbey Church of Saint Denis in 1846.

The mansion was never completed and meanwhile Leigh's fortune was shrinking fast.

After his death in 1873, his son William who had returned from Australia in only the previous year, took over an estate he was unable to finance satisfactorily. He was an extravagant man, and family papers show that his father had to warn him of disheritance unless he changed his life style, whilst his wife, Ada, was an ambitious lady. Put all these facts together and it can readily be seen why the mansion was never finished.

Today it is used for the education of stone masons, and the workmanship and skills employed make it well worth visiting. Horseshoe bats are squatters on the site, taking over at nightfall, whilst cattle and sheep browse contentedly in the fields opposite.

As I write this chapter, I feel a sense of sadness that this monument to the first William Leigh's devotion to his Church and to his family, was never completed, and the house never lived in. What would the bills for heating and lighting have been in this place where even the baths were made of cold Cotswold stone?

The answer must be the same as that given to the buyer contemplating the purchase of a Rolls Royce car. If you have to ask how many miles does it do to the gallon, then you really ought not to be contemplating purchase.

Lest We Forget

There are three war memorials in the manor of Nympsfield and Woodchester that for different reasons are remarkable.

The first to be built was not just the first of the three, but one of the first to be built anywhere in the country for it was consecrated by the Bishop of Clifton on Sunday June 3rd 1917, seventeen months before the Great War ended. It is called the Wayside Cross and stands on the property of the Roman Catholic Church at Woodchester and by the roadside of the A46.

It is an ecumenical memorial recording amongst many other non-Catholics, Richard Jennings, the son of the Rev. Jennings, Rector of Kingstanley. You will also find on the list of names that of George Archer-Shee who was the central character in Terence Rattigan's long-running West End play, The Winslow Boy, and whose story was written by Rodney Bennett in The Archer-Shee's against the Admiralty.

There too is the name of Maurice Dease of the Royal Fusiliers, the first V.C. of the Great War won before the first month was out, in August 1914.

There are one hundred and forty names on the memorial from all over the Stroud district from all religions, and at the consecration ceremony the Rev. Fr. Hugh Pope made that point when he said 'we will inscribe on the base of the Cross the fallen soldiers and sailors of the district'. A very large congregation, estimated at around 5,000, attended the ceremony.

On the Woodchester parish memorial, a solidly sculptured large Cotswold stone of simple design, there are the names of nineteen villagers from the Great War and a further eight from World War II. According to the local weekly paper sixty-nine men went to war from Woodchester, and when one sees the names of those who did not return, and that this was multiplied up and down the country, the horror of war is brought sadly to mind.

At Nympsfield the memorial stands near the crossroads and is made from a piece of war damaged wood brought back from the battlefield near the Somme. A metal sign tells us 'This crucifix, shot and broken, was found on the battlefield of Beugny on the Somme 1917 ...' It stands against the north facing wall of the Chapel House which was once the Red Lion public house where Dr Johnson and Boswell lodged one night when passing through Nympsfield. It was later a village school, and from 1852 the house which the Dominicans had licensed for Catholic worship.

To be a Farmer's Boy

At the time of the Domesday Book (1086) the England we know today had largely been established at least in the names and positions of our communities. Most of our present towns and villages were in existence with the odd exception of Stroud and Nailsworth, neither of which are mentioned in that vast survey.

In rough and ready terms, about one third of England was under forest, and another third under agricultural production. The remaining third was mountain, manorial waste, lakes, rivers, bogland, or early urban development.

There was an old legal phrase 'nulle terre sans seigneur' which implied that all land had a landlord or owner, and from the time of the Norman invasion the country was divided roughly between Crown and Church; the King, and his supporters who received royal grants of manors as payment for their loyalty, and the Church, controlled with rigour from Rome. The Church extracted its annual tithe from all and sundry, and from Saxon times it had a tax called Peter's Pence which was the silver penny coin, and it continued to draw this considerable amount of money back into the Pope's coffers until Henry VIII stopped the practice in 1534.

The manorial system began with the Saxons, and many of the rights of common that operate in parts of the country even today, date back to King Alfred. They have been of the greatest importance to the working man, and have come under pressure and threat from the landowners in every age. Many rights have been lost completely and Nympsfield is one example of this. That Shakespeare was well versed in the country life of Gloucestershire has already been argued but on this particular subject it is Shakespeare again, this time through the voice of Hamlet (Act 1 Scene 4) who sums it up to perfection. In answer to Horatio's question 'Is it a custom?' he replies

> 'Ay, marry is't, but to my mind, – though I am native here,
> And to the manner born, it is a custom,
> More honoured in the breach than in the observance.'

In such a manner were most rights changed and extended, and later lost. Nympsfield is no exception.

The walling of Spring Park now known as Woodchester Park was carried out against commoners rights in the late sixteenth century by Sir George Huntley when he was Lord of the Manor, so that the scene today is very different from what it was in the days of Chaucer. Moreover when Shakespeare wrote Hamlet between 1599 and 1601 it was just after the time Huntley had created his enclosures against the will of the local commoners and their rights. With his knowledge and mention of people and places in Gloucestershire in four other plays, it is surely not unreasonable to suggest that in a fifth play, Hamlet, he is showing once more his grasp of our problems.

We should always bear in mind that agriculture is not an exact science, and for that reason change in farming practice has always been a slow and gradual affair based more on observance of how your neighbour was doing than anything else.

There is also an old saying that necessity is the mother of invention and that farmers would experiment sometimes in desperation in order to balance the books. Such a man of innovation was the first Lord Berkeley who is acclaimed for two changes of farming practice.

The manorial fields under his control were claimed to be the first to be organised by putting strips together and farming under the same system of management; that was in 1243. Two years earlier, in 1241, he is thought to have been the first to attempt to marl the thin Cotswold soil by using a mixture of clay and lime which has a binding effect and aids water retention. Today every groundsman preparing a cricket wicket knows about the use of marl even if he does not use it.

One of the greatest farming innovators in England's history is Jethro Tull (1674–1741) and a claim has been made that he was at some time agent for the Ducie family, but I find that hard to believe. That he was a friend and adviser there can be little doubt, and that the two families exchanged visits is very likely for Tull was brought up on his father's farm in neighbouring Oxfordshire and also farmed Prosperous Farm at nearby Hungerford. However history records that Tull read law at St. John's College, Oxford, and became a barrister at Grays Inn in 1699, and later a bencher. This hardly fits in with duties of running a 4,000 acres estate on a day by day basis as land agent.

Jethro Tull introduced the seed drill and horse-drawn hoe, wrote a book on horse-hoe husbandry, and his advice on producing a finer tilth and oxygenation from various methods of cultivation was widely followed. His methods spread to France through his friendship with the French political philosopher Voltaire during the latter's exile here between 1726 and 1729. In this district Tull's methods were adopted, in particular his recommendation of the use of sainfoin with its deep tap root, ideal for Cotswold uplands.

Those who visit the Coaley Peak Picnic Site in mid-summer should look for a pink flowered vetch-like plant in flower at the same time as the yellow Common Rattle. When you see it remember its part in our local history.

As one who regularly walks Selsley Common, Coaley Peak, and Uley Bury, I can recommend the area to wild flower lovers. In the three months of May, June and July one can count between twenty and thirty plants in flower on any day excluding the grasses, and by their study to understand how the fallow field would have provided food for grazing animals, especially at the headlands.

Old common pasture is not in the same league as modern ley mixtures for producing quantity and heavy crops, but its broad spectrum of natural minerals and the obvious relish with which it is grazed shows it is of considerable nutritional value.

Lord Ducie of Moreton, who died in 1735 was a friend and follower of Jethro Tull. He was also an innovator and was the first in the county to use the turnip, which gave the third year break in the farming system, and also gave an autumn feed after a barley or winter wheat harvest. It was developed by Viscount Townshend (1675–1738) of Rainham in Norfolk who lived at the same time as Tull and Ducie. He was nicknamed Turnip for his pains, but there can be little doubt that the use of this root crop and the fact it could be grazed in situ meant a great deal to English agriculture coming when it did at the turn of the c17 and c18.

The old farming system was based on a two-field design: one field wheat and one field fallow. The fallow field meant weeds, couch grass, and poa annua grazed off by sheep and cattle, who went into the other field after harvest to eat up the gleanings whilst the fallow field was prepared for sowing the next season's crop. The variation to this was the three-field system of two grain and one fallow, allowing a crop of oats or barley along with the wheat, but that came later, and Minchinhampton and Shipton Moyne were the first on the Cotswold uplands to operate that system.

Arguably the most vital part of the manorial system was the common pasture or manorial waste. This was the common land outside the two or three arable fields where every householder had rights of common.

Amongst these rights were pannage which allowed cottagers to graze their pigs on acorns or beech mast under the woods at Buckholt which are centuries old. This would have provided only a supplementary feed, not to be relied on annually, for only one year in four gave a good crop. Nevertheless it was of great help to the cottager, for the pig being the quickest converter of vegetation into meat of any animal, was the main source of animal protein on which to raise a family.

As William Cobbett wrote in 'Rural Rides' in 1826: 'a pig in every cottage sty; that is the infallible mark of a happy people.'

A further advantage of the pig is that everything about it has value: chitterling, Bath chaps, and trotters are good wholesome foods, as too are hams and bacons kept for long periods by a process of curing of which the local Wiltshire was most popular. Sides of bacon would also be smoked and let hang in the cottage chimneys for use over winter. Bones would be stewed for stock and soup, and the marrow extracted, and finally the bones were ground up for fertiliser.

The Cotswold practice of keeping a sow and rearing an average litter of eight offspring in a stone sty at the bottom of the garden, was one which has only died out in recent years.

During World War II most villages had a Pig Club which organised the collection and communal boiling of swill from leftovers of kitchens and gardens, and arranged for a monthly delivery of pig food against each cottager's ration cards. Food rationing did not end until 1954, but for another decade and a half the practice of pig rearing and fattening continued, and was for many a profitable sideline as well as a hobby.

Nympsfield was one such village.

An advantage Nympsfield had over some of its neighbours was that in the centre of the village off Front Street behind Cotswold House there was a bacon factory at one time operated by members of the Witchell family who first arrived in 1745. This would have made the task of getting the home produced pig turned into food for the family so much easier and probably would have been an encouragement for pigs to be kept in the first place. Sadly it provided an enormous hygiene problem for the blood and effluent filtered into the natural spring water and Nympsfield did not get piped water until 1940.

As for the other rights of common, piscary may have been claimed after the establishment of the fish ponds in Woodchester Park in the eighteenth century, but by then the lands there had long been enclosed so it is unlikely. The most important would have been the rights of estover or housebote where the commoner could collect wood for house building and repair, and for the making of implements. Finally he had the right to collect wood for fuel provided it was fallen wood which could be picked up off the ground. Tradition has it that one did this 'by hook or by crook' meaning by any means: thus by the use of his hook he might help a branch fall to the ground where it would be gathered together by the crook. Correct or not it is a likely tale of the way countryfolk find a way around rules. Without this right one can imagine the despair and suffering to both the poor people and their animals in the early part of 1607 when the winter was so bitterly cold that the River Severn froze over at Tewkesbury. At such times it is easy to follow the words of Thomas Tusser when he wrote

> From Christmas to May
> Weak cattle decay.

In the middle of that spell came the Lenten fast before each Easter which has been described as a period in time combining virtue with necessity. As we sit in our double-glazed centrally heated houses, with carpets wall to wall, in the glow of electric lighting, and when so many recent winters have been mild with hardly a flake of snow about, it is hard to picture the grim harshness of a Cotswold cottage at Townsend two hundred years ago when my great great grandfather Richard Smith was a teenager. He was just starting work as an agricultural labourer. The year was 1798 and we were at war with France.

The combination of losing manpower to the Army and the Royal Navy, and the demands on labour of the cloth manufacturers who were then at their peak providing uniforms and blankets, meant that there were vacancies in the farming industry. From this moment on the Smith family left their background of tradesmen – cordwainers, sawyers, blacksmiths, weavers – and entered the world of agriculture.

It has to be like with like

It was only when I started to write about the most common of all trades, and looked back on the changes over the past two or three centuries in agriculture and how it affected the lives of my forebears in and around Nympsfield, that I realised that a chapter on weights and measures had to be written.

We have all accepted these changes and they have gradually taken over, and nobody has put it all down on paper so that proper comparisons can now be made: unless this is written down you cannot compare like with like, and all comparisons are meaningless.

Look up any old map and it will tell you the scale on which it has been drawn up; so many miles to the inch.

Read the Victoria History of any county and it will be subdivided into chapters covering each hundred.

Farmers will still speak about the acreage they farm and the gallons each cow produces, but their children are referring to hectares and litres; before long, as with the quantities purchased at the petrol pump, the old measures will be taken over by the new and in years to come another generation will not be able to compare like with like once again.

Before all this is drowned in a metricated sea it would be as well to look back at the old measures so that we may understand some of the facts in the history books.

Recently whilst inspecting the site where Park Mill existed at the bottom dam on the bottom lake in Woodchester Park along with Dr. Ray Collins of the Gloucestershire Industrial Archaeology Society, old papers were produced referring to 'loads of grain' and 'bushels of wheat'. I have to confess that neither of us knew and we can partly be excused in that both phrases refer to a volumetric measurement. Water is a constant density so a bushel of water weighs 80 lbs, but wheat is not a constant and the weight will be decided by quality and moisture content. The average weight of a bushel of wheat of good quality and not in excess of 16% moisture is 63 lbs, but it will be noticed that there are qualifications in the definition.

In measurements what about a hide or a virgate; a rod, pole, or perch; a chain or a furlong?

Most of these words come from the Old English or even Norman French, and superseded Saxon words. The old Saxon mark is still in use in Germany but has disappeared in England.

The Bishop of Worcester in whose diocese Nympsfield lay in Norman times, ordered a pension of two marks from the churches of Quenington and Nympsfield to the Abbot of St. Peter's, Gloucester, but that statement is meaningless in modern terms.

The land measurements are perhaps the most interesting for they dovetail together in a very logical way.

The foot describes a vague length relating to the human foot, and the inch was a twelfth part of that measurement; a yard of three feet was a human step or pace. These became established as set lengths for uniformity.

Two actual measures from these were the chain, and the rod, pole, or perch. The chain was the length of a team of oxen, and was the length therefore of the lead rein by which the team was controlled by the driver or ploughman, and covered twenty-two yards. The rod or pole or perch was a quarter of a chain being five and half yards or sixteen and a half feet. Fascinatingly the rod is both a word used for centuries in fishing, and also the traditional length of a fishing rod used in some Irish loughs where dapping for trout is still carried on when the mayfly is up.

All this fits like a glove into the manorial farming system and much since. The rod or pole was used to mark out the walls of a cottage which was two rods by one rod (11 yards × $5^{1}/_{2}$ yards). The cottager who lived within, had a strip of farmland called simply a land, which was a furrow long, or furlong of 220 yards, and the width of this land was the rod or pole of 5½ yards. The ploughman turned the topsoil in one direction the width of two lands or half a chain so that it was one chain of twenty-two yards between each ridge and likewise each furrow. The area covered by ploughing four lands or between each furrow peaked by its ridge was called an acre (one furlong × one chain, or 4840 square yards).

There are very few fields left of this design; the need to produce all the home-grown food we could during World War II to save our shipping, meant that most were ploughed up at that time and returned to an arable rotation.

<........22 yards or 1 chain........>

FURROW   RIDGE   FURROW   RIDGE   FURROW

Dr. J.A. Venn, the agricultural historian and economist, held the view that the game of cricket which retains the length of a cricket wicket at one chain or twenty-two yards, owes much in its origins to the manorial farming system.

Young boys would be employed in bird scaring after ploughing and seeding the arable strips, and as boredom crept in, would throw stones at targets from ridge to ridge that eventually would be defended by a stick or wooden cudgel, and so were the rudiments of cricket created.

Mention has been made of virgates, hides, and hundreds.

A virgate was thirty acres, and there were four virgates to a hide. At Domesday it was recorded that there were three hides or 360 acres at Nympsfield. A hundred meant a hundred hides, so here we are talking about 12,000 acres. Nympsfield stood at the joining point near Coaley Peak of three separate hundreds – Langtree, Whitstone and Berkeley which would have totalled around 36,000 acres.

After World War II the corn trade was a world that no longer exists. We still had regular corn markets at Mark Lane in London, and regionally at the Corn Exchange in Corn Street in Bristol. Here samples were examined, smelt, felt, bitten and chewed, and the dealers on the floor made their bids and bartered. Outside the exchange in Corn Street, Bristol, the black metal stands with circular flat top called nails still exist where cash was handled and counted, and the phrase 'pay on the nail' implying a spot cash transaction, entered the English language. Grain merchants sit now behind computers and buy and sell by the shipload.

The bushels had already gone but as bulk transport was in its infancy grain was still moved in sacks. The company names of Gopsill Brown and West of England Sack Contractors, who hired out and repaired grain sacks, linger in the memory. They produced sacks of the same size, which meant that wheat being the densest variety weighed heavier per sack than barley or oats. A sack of wheat weighed two and a quarter hundredweights (252 lbs); a sack of barley was the easy measure at two hundredweights (224 lbs and twenty sacks to the ton); oats gave one and a half hundredweights per sack (168 lbs). Fortunately the weights dovetailed into the monetary system: a ton was 20 cwts and a pound sterling 20 shillings. If you bought grain at 15/– per cwt you knew instantly that was £15 per ton.

There is one more weight that was fast disappearing from the scene just after the last War to which reference must be made because it links with the bushel and is the most confusing of all: that is the quarter.

This is not a quarter of a ton or hundredweight: this was a measure of eight bushels. In this at least there was some logic, for eight bushels of wheat at 63lbs totalled 504lbs, or exactly four and half hundredweights. There the logic ended, because if you multiply that quarter by four you end up with eighteen hundredweights, not a ton of twenty hundredweights. If you got that wrong you would make or lose a lot of money.

Sheep, Wool, and Cloth: A Staple Industry

'My days are swifter than a weaver's shuttle, and we are spent without hope'
                        Book of Job, Chap 7. Verse 6
                              4th–6th century BC

From the days of Chaucer in the 14th century for five hundred years until the nineteenth century the production of wool and the manufacture of cloth was England's greatest trade.

For over four hundred years most of that cloth making was a cottage industry. The work of carding, spinning and weaving was put out to cottagers in the villages and some of Nympsfield's buildings are living memorials to those times and that industry. The houses in Back Street past the Rose & Crown show where broadcloth weaving was carried out. The large window frames in that row of houses are reminders of the importance of daylight in the operation. A visit to Ebley and Stanley Mills will give examples of how the daylight design principle was used in the cloth mills, especially by the architect G. F. Bodley in his rebuild of Ebley Mill, nowadays the offices of Stroud District Council. Two other fine square Cotswold stone houses in Front Street were also known weaver's homes, but the industry was so widespread that many other cottages ill-suited for the task would have been used in the hopes of making a living.

This cottage industry should not be understated. Farming and forestry provided food and warmth and the skills to make housing and tools for trades. Making cloth for yourself and your family was the other major need of an isolated village community and cloth manufacture was never far behind. It developed quite naturally out of the other two occupations.

The competition for labour after the Black Death saw the first major switch in farming from arable to grassland, and the development of cattle and sheep husbandry. The average weight of cattle at Smithfield doubled between 1710 and 1795, and so did the population, so demand and supply kept in balance. The increase in sheep however meant more wool to be sheared and sold, and an important side-effect of bigger flocks meant the physical advantages of the sheep treading the thin Cotswold brash with the 'golden hoof' and adding valuable natural fertiliser to the soil. In consequence the arable crops were larger, there was extra meat for the table, and finally there was resort to home-made cloth and a thriving cottage industry.

In case this gives the impression of instant prosperity one should add that farming has never been the source of overnight fortunes except perhaps by property sales.

There was also fierce competition at every stage of cloth manufacture, and in the early years the 'putting-out' system saw the birth of the entrepreneur who did not own a mill but was the organiser and planner, the merchant who had to know his markets, the buyer of spun wool from the cottage spinner, and the man who risked his capital by owning the material being handled through every process. He moved with the tide of demand and supply and became the middleman between the cottage industry and the finishing done by the earlier mills and later still, the clothier himself.

Such a man around 1700 was Jonathan Witchell, and amongst the later clothiers who invested wisely and well were the Sheppards at Uley, the Playnes at Avening, the Marlings at Selsley, Ebley, and Kingstanley, the Pauls at Woodchester, and the Austins at Wotton under Edge.

The last named family was a force in the county for many years, but even with them they reached the heights and plumbed the depths inside a generation. In 1801 they employed 195 workers but were dissolved in 1811. George Austin formed a new company in the same year but died insolvent four years later in 1815. In the January of 1815 Richard Smith married Mary Austin in St. Bartholomew's Church Nympsfield (See family tree, Appendix A).

The family continued under a partnership of E.E. & A. Austin which involved itself in the risky banking business of those days, giving extended credit to a large number of retail outlets, and paying interest on many loans which were then used as cashflow to remain in business. In 1830 a meeting of creditors brought the precarious finances out into the open. In the twenty years from 1812, 139 country tailors and retailers had been bankrupted, and clearly the post Napoleonic War depression took a heavy toll not only on the Austins but throughout the cloth industry. The Austins folded finally in 1832, and were followed by Edward Sheppard in 1837. This was the same Sheppard who had built from his earlier profits, the Gatcombe Park estate now owned by Princess Anne.

Between 1820 and 1841, sixty mills in Gloucestershire ceased working, and in the same period the population of Uley fell by 900 and that of Wotton by 780. In 1833, Lewis of Ebley Oil Mill said that his father 'made as much profit on one cloth as I do by twenty'. By 1856 there were no mills working cloth at Uley or Dursley, and only one at Cam and one at Wotton. The Cam mill is still in operation today.

In the good days of broadcloth weaving, the weaver was a king amongst his fellow workers. In 1814 at the end of the long war against France, he earned two guineas (£2.10) for a six day week compared with 45p for a farmworker. It is hard to translate these figures into modern terms, although the twelve hour day is simple enough to understand and for us to consider unbearable.

As for the money, a leaflet on free trade dated 1847 and referring to the cloth industry stated that 'many accumulated sufficient property and income ... to live in comfort', The Gloucester Journal reported in 1819, the year my great grandfather Moses Smith was born, that a broadcloth weaver in Painswick had left in his will, £50 for Gloucester Infirmary. That would perhaps be the equivalent of a £3000 bequest today, and we would all murmur about the generosity of the modern artisan in reading of it. Clearly then just over two pounds a week around 1820 was no hardship, and it is little wonder that most villages had a pub for every ten houses and saw them full.

The saying 'as drunk as a lord' dates back to the reign of George III (1760–1820) and through the first half of the nineteenth century the acceptable role model to be followed was the man who could afford to drink heavily in public: it was the sign of a gentleman. It was a situation that led to great hardship and suffering in many households, and brought the temperance movement into active operation throughout England in the nineteenth century.

The volatility of nineteenth-century life was further affected by the increase in population in these islands. At the 1801 Census, the first accurate check on population, there were 10.4 millions in Great Britain, 5.2 millions in Ireland, and remarkably just 5.3 millions in the U.S.A. Forty years later in 1841 Great Britain had gone up to 18,534,000, Ireland to 8,175,000, and U.S.A. to 17,063,353. The tragic years of the potato famine in 1845–48 decimated the Irish figures by a quarter whilst Great Britain moved on to nearly twenty-one millions. Small pox had been killing one person in fourteen in every year, but the discovery of a vaccination by the Berkeley physician Dr. Jenner (1749–1823) was to alter medical thinking radically. Later in the century Louis Pasteur (1822–95) led the way with the attack on the tuberculosis bacillus in milk, and gave his name to the method pasteurisation. He also provided vaccinations against anthrax and rabies. Then there was Lister (1827–1912) the founder of antiseptic medicine. The new methods and an increasing understanding of the importance of hygiene had an enormous effect on life expectancy and on population size.

All this increase in population took place at the same time that so many were emigrating. Seventy-eight people left Uley for Canada in 1835, and in the same year around two hundred left for Australia from Horsley, Kingscote, Uley, Owlpen, the Stanleys, Avening, Minchinhampton and Kingswood. In 1840 common land was enclosed for the use as allotments in Uley, Horsley and Nailsworth, land which had formerly been used for pasturing donkeys and ponies used to carry wool, yarn and cloth.

One of the mills owned and leased for cloth manufacture by the Austin family in 1824 was Huntingford Mill which in more recent years was operated in the corn trade by G & M Durn: this unusually was a father and daughter partnership of Gilbert and Mary Durn who traded successfully for many years after World War II in the Berkeley Vale.

Probably from 1780 to 1815 were the peak years for the West of England cloth trade centred around the Stroud district, but by this one must not infer that it was all downhill thereafter. The Marling family had the confidence and the ability to invest at the beginning of the nineteenth century, and living at Stanley Park, Selsley they were neighbours of all who lived at Nympsfield, Uley and Owlpen as well as Woodchester on the southern slopes of the same hill.

The Marlings also are credited with the building of the last of the Cotswold wool churches at Selsley: the Church of All Saints. Designed by G.F. Bodley shortly after completing his apprenticeship under Sir George Gilbert Scott it shows clearly the fashion for Gothic revivalist architecture followed by Scott and his friend Augustus Pugin. It was built in 1862 and Bodley whose promise of commissions had encouraged William Morris to set up his firm, Morris, Marshall, Faulkner & Co gave them their first contract at Selsley to make the stained glass windows which are such a delight to all who visit the church. It was the same Marling family that was instrumental in founding the secondary school that carries to this day the family name as its title. Marling School was founded in 1887 and is a Grant Maintained Grammar Technical School at this time.

So clearly it was not all doom and gloom in the West of England cloth trade through to the twentieth century.

As the end of the second millennium approaches there is no British owned firm left in the cloth trade around Stroud. Two mills remain: at the former Strachans mills of Lodgemoor and Fromehall at the western entrance to the town of Stroud itself, and at the former Hunt & Winterbotham mill at Cam. In my youth there was a third mill in the same group named Winterbotham Strachan and Playne, and that was the Playne family mill at Avening. They were taken over by the Yorkshire company Illingworth, Morris and are now owned by an American company, Milliken. No woollen or worsted cloths for suitings are now made; the basic two fabrics produced are tennis ball outers, and the green baize for snooker tables. The spinning and weaving is done at Cam, and finished at Stroud.

Unable to meet the profit margins expected by their American owners and their Japanese consultants, 'the finest cloth in the world,' as it was once claimed, with a shop in London's Golden Square, and another on the QE2, is no longer in production. The broadcloth weavers handling their shuttles at Nympsfield seem a planet away.

The Bristol and Gloucestershire Gliding Club

Bladud, the son of a British king named Lud Hudibras was a leper and was expelled from his father's court. Living in the valley of the River Avon in what we now know as north Somerset he wandered around and became a swineherd or pig keeper. The pigs are said to have contracted leprosy from Bladud but after rolling in some stagnating warm mud were healed. Presumably Bladud did the same and was also cured for he returned to his father's court and was readily accepted back. Bladud later went back to the place where he was cured and there built the city of Bath in 863 BC and the news of the warm mineral waters soon spread.

The famous Pump Room in Bath was built in 1700 and an inscription recording this legend is to be found there.

If that was not enough to preserve his name in the annals of history Bladud decided that even if his pigs could not fly, at least he would make an attempt, and this he did in 852 BC, and so history records him for a second remarkable event. He 'toke upon hym to flie into y ayer' but sadly it was not a success and he sustained fatal injuries.

At least the story makes two points: it shows that the West of England has always been in the van of man's attempts to fly and that those attempts began nearly three thousand years ago.

The Bristol Gliding Club was formed in 1938 and operated from a field at Leighterton from which Lord Apsley who was the club's President, used to fly his own light aircraft. War put an end to civil gliding the following year, and both Lord Apsley and one of the Vice-Presidents, Captain Barnwell lost their lives flying during the war. Air Commodore Egbert Cadbury became the new President, and the club searched urgently for a new base as Leighterton was not suitable. In 1955 Longridge Farm, Nympsfield, owned by L.J. Dalby and farmed by his daughter and son in law became available and the deal was made.

In 1957 Peter Scott the artist and head of the Severn Wildfowl Trust at Slimbridge, joined the club, and within four years became National Champion in 1961. In 1990 his widow Lady Phillipa Scott opened the Sir Peter Scott extension at the clubhouse at Longridge.

Today there are two hundred and thirty flying members.

The Parish Pump

Look after the pennies, the pounds will look after themselves. In politics see that the parish pump is in good working order and the country will be in good heart. For those who may consider that Britain has not had the benefit of good governance for most of this century, it will come as no surprise to know that Nympsfield has had a long problem with the parish pump.

The subject of an acceptable water supply and the need for good drains and sewerage has taken up much time at parish meetings, and if one needed proof of the saying 'the mills of God grind exceeding slow' then it is to be found here.

When the Great War broke out in August 1914 twenty-four volunteered and only fifteen returned, but they left behind them a problem that would take many years to resolve. In 1914 the parish meeting debated the need for drains and decided that none were wanted. It was claimed that the bacon factory off Front Street was the cause, and that blood and other liquid matter was fouling the natural springs, and coming out at the Four Wells on the Plain which was the main water supply. Twenty-one years later in 1935 the pollution had reached the stage where the English answer to most problems was adopted: a committee was formed. The chairman was the Rev. Williams and its members were Messrs Heaven, Mills, Pearce, Pitcher, and Smith. They proposed that water and sewerage should be connected to Uley and a letter sent to Dursley Rural District Council stating without equivocation that the water was unfit for drinking. The Dursley councillors turned down the application, so it was a further five years later at the start of the second world war in 1940 that Nympsfield got connected. A further three years later in 1943 the water supply was extended to Cockadilly.

In Ron Easton's fascinating essay on a century of parish affairs, there are many other gems to enjoy.

It was in 1896 that the Vicar of St. Bartholomew's, the Rev James Silvester chaired the parish meeting at which Emmanuel Mills proposed and John Smith seconded his nomination as District Councillor. That was the way you got elected in 1896. No waste of time canvassing and knocking on doors and wearing out shoe leather: no ballot box and no secret votes.

1899 saw a debate on the spelling of Nympsfield but that has already been covered in this book.

The Parish Council was formed in 1938 and the first Council was J. Clew, H. Mills, T. H. Mills, and A. J. Mills along with the Rev. Williams. The parish meeting continued until 1953 and the longest serving clerk was John Mills (1894–1930) who died in office.

An outbreak of diphtheria struck the village in 1938 and twelve children were taken to the isolation hospital at Over near Gloucester.

Electricity was another advance that took up debating time. As with water the 1945 Council meeting was told to wait three years, and no doubt in some frustration, in 1948 they passed a proposal that the clerk 'should purchase a suitable lamp for Council meetings'. Presumably that would have been an oil lamp but at least they got value from the purchase for it was 1955 before electricity arrived. The wheel then turned full circle for the R. A. Lister factory in the village was still using a diesel powered engine to make its own electricity – one of its own manufacture – and complaints were made about the vibration caused and the company asked to switch to the National Grid.

In December 1998 the last outpost of oil-fired lighting converted to electricity when to the great delight of the media if not to the Watts family, Sheepcote Farm finally surrendered.

The Village Today

Nympsfield lies on top of the Cotswold Hills at just 800 feet above sea level at its highest point at Stonehill, and has magnificent views in most directions. Just over a quarter of a mile to the north west of the village at Coaley Peak Picnic Site, as well as at Stonehill, there is a view of breathtaking beauty across the Severn Valley and the Royal Forest of Dean into the high peaks of the Black Mountains and the Brecon Beacons, to May Hill in Gloucestershire, and to the Malverns in Worcestershire. After rain has cleared the air, and the warm summer sun has picked out distant peaks, you would not wish to be anywhere else.

In winter, an east wind blowing straight from the North Sea and the Baltic, has the cutting edge of a Russian snow scene, for there is no higher land between Nympsfield and those far-off places.

As a local member of the Flat Earth Society would put it: 'On a clear day you can see them Urals'.

Take a cursory glance around, and there is nothing special about this upland village. The soil is limestone brash, thin soil mixed with small stones just a spit's depth, which normally means sheep and barley. Yet dairy farming, fields of wheat and potatoes, crops of elder flower for the bottled soft drinks market, and even organic market gardening play their full part nowadays.

The village that once boasted five inns, The Bell, The Red Lion, The Rose & Crown, The Red Bull, and the White Hart has now just one, The Rose & Crown ideally placed at the junction of Front Street and Back Street, and on the main road through the village, to be the coaching house it was in the old days. It has not always been called the Rose & Crown: for two hundred years it was called the Ducie Arms in deference to the then Lord of the Manor, the Earl of Ducie. It is built in traditional Cotswold style with mullioned and transomed windows and is nearly four hundred years old dating back to the early seventeenth century.

The Post Office has moved from its earlier site and is now part of a modern bungalow and sells newspapers on weekdays. The primary school is run by the Roman Catholics under the LEA, and draws its pupils from a wide area, and in 1938 had the author Evelyn Waugh on its board of managers. There are two churches, St. Bartholomew's Church of England, and St. Joseph's Roman Catholic Church. The Nonconformist community, which had an active Baptist Chapel rebuilt in 1760 in Townsend, now has to go out of the village to Shortwood for its services.

The general stores run for so many years by Jack Neale in Back Street near the Barrow is now closed, but the house is still occupied by his daughter Patricia.

Cows are no longer milked at Court Farm for Jack Wooldridge has semi-retired, and as an octogenarian he now restricts himself to helping out with the calves. His sons have built new buildings in Davids Lane in which to milk the one hundred and twenty cows. The Court Farm buildings date back to 1617.

Mary Wooldridge no longer looks after the poultry and has moved to a new bungalow opposite Cotswold House in Front Street, at the back of which was the bacon factory once owned by the Witchell family and more recently by the Walkleys.

Like much else this is no more. A thriving printing business, the Nimsfielde Press, which gallantly carried on the tradition of spelling the village name in its title without y, p, or h, has now also closed its doors, but the premises are happily occupied by a firm specialising in photocopiers run by Mike Reynolds. Street Farm in Front Street is no longer involved in farming.

A Pegler and a Mills still farm in or near the village, and a Neale family live in it as already mentioned, but the Burfords,

Bushells, Phipps, Daniels, Witchells, Fishers, Whites, Hodges, and Rodmans, the Adeys, Hines, Browns, and Preens, with all of whom my forebears were intermarried, have all gone. In the churchyard of St. Bartholomews Church there are seven marked and two unmarked graves of Smiths, seven Mills, six Neale's, five Burfords, and four Daniels.

This is all very much in the past, for my grandparents were married in Nympsfield in 1876 and then left and were buried in Ebley; my great grandfather Moses Smith returned only to be married to Mary Ann Mills for his second marriage in 1881; and finally after living most of her life in Gloucester, my grand Aunt, Harriet Pegler was brought back to be buried in St. Bartholomews Church in 1913, and that was the last direct link.

There is no village pond near the Barrow any more for the visiting mallard or swan to enjoy, and the name the Barrow is all that remains of a tumulus that once existed in the heart of Nympsfield.

Not many villages can boast two current University Professors and a University Lecturer but Nympsfield can. John King is Professor of Animal Breeding at Edinburgh, Peter Hennessey is Professor of Contemporary History at London, and Guy Watts lectures in the English faculty at Turin. The last two started at St. Josephs, and all three went to Marling.

Nor should we forget another St. Joseph's and Marling product, Anthony Wooldridge who won a scholarship to Oxford and is now back in Gloucestershire doing research work at Berkeley. Finally I mention Zoe Crossland who is doing research in archaeology for a Ph.D. at the University of Michigan which she reached via St. Joseph's and Cambridge.

There is a fine community spirit in the village well shown by the two churches joining happily together for the Harvest Festival and Christmas Carol Service celebrations held each year in St. Bartholomew's Church. It is also demonstrated when each year the village enters the Heart of England Britain in Bloom competition, and in 1997 and again in 1998 it challenged successfully, winning the village category. The village was organised and led by Ann Overton, the wife of Bob Overton, a retired Clifton College housemaster, and she also won the Interflora Trophy for her efforts in the competition.

In 1998 the judges entered eight regional winners from around the United Kingdom in a national competition, and in the village category, Nympsfield won the second prize.

This was a remarkable performance because the winner was Bray in Berkshire with a population of nine thousand people, and a budget of £38,000. Nympsfield has a population of just over three hundred, and entered thanks to the support of many small sponsors and a cheque for £500 from the Stroud District Council. It was very much a team effort both in the raising of funds and also the physical work involved. Special thanks should be recorded in addition, to valued guidance and advice of a professional landscape gardener, Joe Rayner; to the Parish Council under the chairmanship of Rose Westwood; and to the staff and children of St. Joseph's School.

The schoolchildren gained educational value from the exercise, started their efforts from seeds, and learned the meaning of green fingers.

In 1999 the villagers are aiming for the hat trick. A good time to see Nympsfield in bloom will be in July, but don't rule out June and August.

Summer is also a good time for visitors interested in history with Uley Bury, Hetty Pegler's Tump, Owlpen Manor, Selsley Common and the Toots, and Woodchester Park Mansion the main attractions.

For the more adventurous the Bristol and Gloucestershire Gliding Club provides for enthusiasts one of the premier sites in the United Kingdom, and both at Selsley Common and Coaley Peak intrepid youth launches itself off the Cotswold escarpment enjoying the view from a hang-glider.

Nympsfield as you can see, is changing like many another village, sometimes for the better, sometimes for the worse. It could do with a general stores again, for the isolation of a century past could well be felt by the old, the sick, the poor, and the very young, as petrol prices rise inexorably, and buses get rarer. The supermarkets are great for those with cars, and the deep pockets to splash out on the variety of choice they provide but they are not always the cheapest.

It could perhaps do with a café or tea rooms, for the nearest is at the Pumps in Uley. There is no longer a cricket eleven in the name of Nympsfield but the King George V playing field still provides a site for soccer and a nomad team uses the cricket square occasionally in the summer, so there are still outlets for sporting prowess.

The Working Men's Club was formed in 1898 and has therefore just completed its centenary. It had begun life as a Reading Room open every evening from 1895, but three years later was granted a licence to provide tobacco and beer, and has been doing so successfully ever since. Its mock Tudor façade faces the Maris Convent on Front Street.

In many ways Nympsfield is a typical English village: it hates change. Nevertheless today's village is vastly different from that of a hundred years ago, and a glance through the chapter on the deliberations of the Parish Council shows how solid was the opposition to the changes that did take place. In his final chapter of 'Cider with Rosie', Laurie Lee wrote that he

> 'belonged to that generation which saw, by chance, the end of a thousand years' life'.

He could have been writing about Nympsfield, or indeed Uley, Frocester, Selsley, Woodchester.

Nympsfield then is not alone, and as you stroll along its lanes, you sense the atmosphere of a place at peace with itself. Well... almost.

Did someone mention windpower?

Appendix A

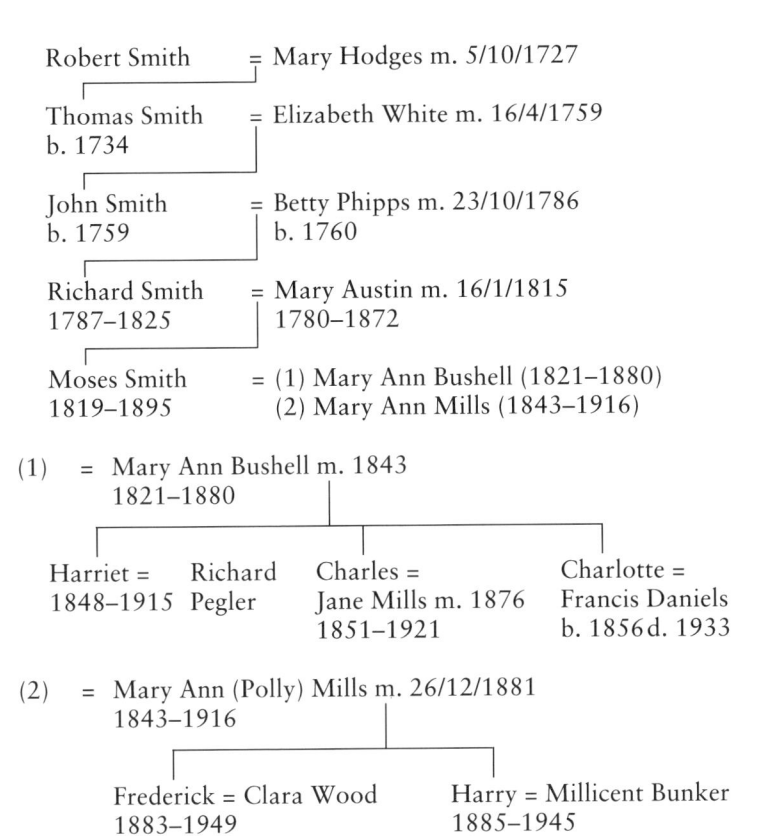

```
Robert Smith      = Mary Hodges m. 5/10/1727
│
Thomas Smith      = Elizabeth White m. 16/4/1759
b. 1734
│
John Smith        = Betty Phipps m. 23/10/1786
b. 1759             b. 1760
│
Richard Smith     = Mary Austin m. 16/1/1815
1787–1825           1780–1872
│
Moses Smith       = (1) Mary Ann Bushell (1821–1880)
1819–1895           (2) Mary Ann Mills (1843–1916)
```

(1) = Mary Ann Bushell m. 1843
      1821–1880

- Harriet = Richard Pegler
  1848–1915
- Charles = Jane Mills m. 1876
  1851–1921
- Charlotte = Francis Daniels
  b. 1856 d. 1933

(2) = Mary Ann (Polly) Mills m. 26/12/1881
      1843–1916

- Frederick = Clara Wood
  1883–1949
- Harry = Millicent Bunker
  1885–1945

This is a pollarded tree with some branches lopped off, but it does show the Smith connection with Nympsfield as far back as can be proved. All six generations are Nympsfield by direct connection. It also shows the old Liberal Party connection in the last two generations: Charles Smith served on the Mid-Gloucestershire Liberal Council, Francis Daniels was a Liberal on the Birmingham City Council, and Harry Smith was a Liberal for the Eastgate Ward of Gloucester City Council. The author stood for the Liberal Party in the 1966 General Election in the Stroud constituency.

From Robert Smith who was born around 1700 to my grandson Kieron Smith are ten generations.

Appendix B

The Ducie family came first from Little Aston, Staffordshire, and the marriage of Henry with Mary Hardy was in 1571 during the reign of Queen Elizabeth I, when he was a banker in London. The first baronet was his son Robert who was banker to the Royal family and King Charles I. Sir Robert became Lord Mayor of London, bought the manor of Tortworth – the first appearance in Gloucestershire – and died in 1634.

His fourth son Robert was still managing the home estate of Little Aston but by his marriage to Mary Lowe of Ozleworth in Gloucestershire, the granddaughter of Sir Thomas Lowe who had also been Lord Mayor of London in 1604, the line was kept alive but through the distaff. Their daughter Elizabeth by her marriage to Edward Moreton brought that family name into the genealogy. Moreton was a man of Staffordshire no doubt through the Little Aston connection met Elizabeth Ducie. Their son Matthew Ducie Moreton was created the first Baron Ducie of Moreton, and his son, also Matthew, who was second Baron Ducie of Moreton became the first Baron Ducie of Tortworth but died unmarried in 1770. The titles were kept alive in the Ducie name by a legal arrangement whereby his Reynolds nephews assuming the arms and surname of Moreton. Disappointment followed in that the next holder of the title Thomas Reynolds Moreton also died without issue in 1785. He had married Margaret Ramsden the daughter of Sir John Ramsden from Yorkshire. His successor was a Captain in the Royal Navy, Francis Reynolds Moreton, and it was his son Thomas who was created the first Earl of Ducie. He died in 1840. Henry George Francis Reynolds Moreton then became the second Earl of Ducie and it was he who sold the Woodchester Park estate and returned to the family home at Tortworth.

By coincidence living and working in Nympsfield is Mike Reynolds who told me his family came from Aston. Of course this may be just a coincidence but Reynolds is an uncommon surname and there is the place name as well: he should research his family tree.

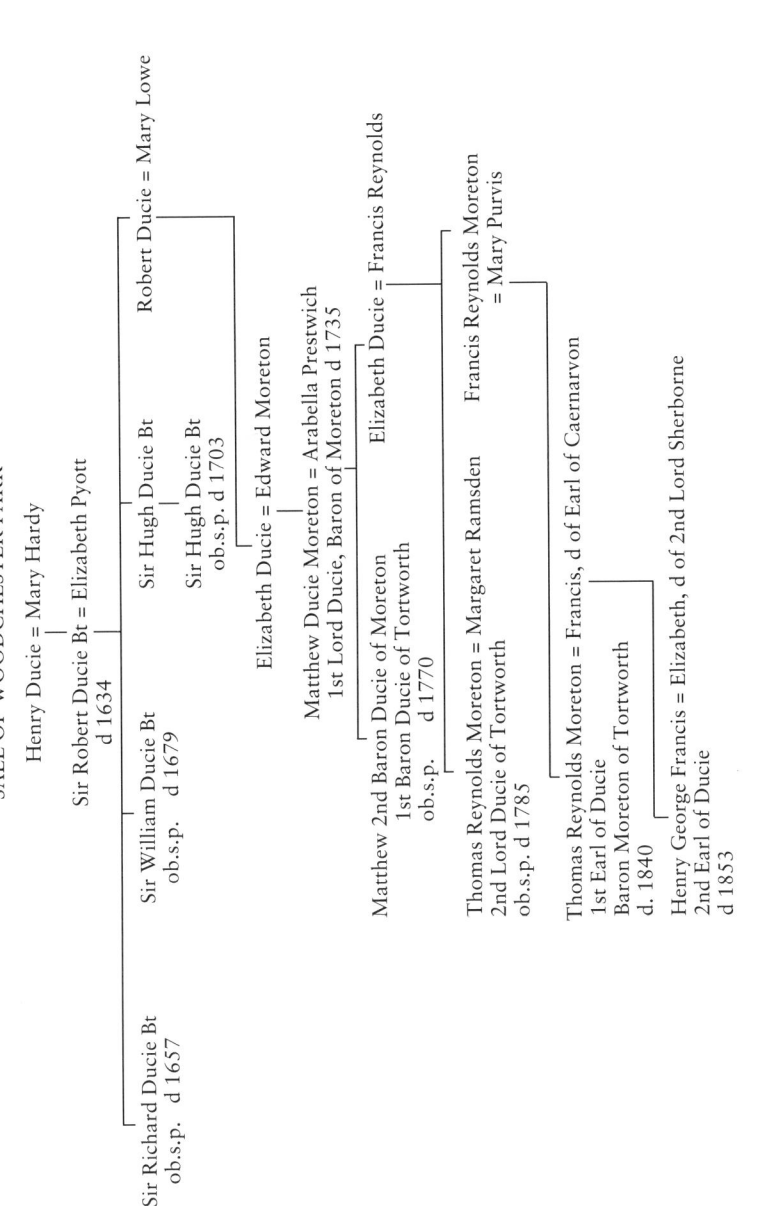

THE GENEALOGY OF THE DUCIE FAMILY FROM THE FIRST BARONETCY TO THE EARL OF DUCIE AT THE TIME OF SALE OF WOODCHESTER PARK

Henry Ducie = Mary Hardy

Sir Robert Ducie Bt = Elizabeth Pyott
d 1634

- Sir Richard Ducie Bt
  ob.s.p. d 1657
- Sir William Ducie Bt
  ob.s.p. d 1679
- Sir Hugh Ducie Bt
  |
  Sir Hugh Ducie Bt
  ob.s.p. d 1703
- Robert Ducie = Mary Lowe

Elizabeth Ducie = Edward Moreton

Matthew Ducie Moreton = Arabella Prestwich
1st Lord Ducie, Baron of Moreton d 1735

- Matthew 2nd Baron Ducie of Moreton
  1st Baron Ducie of Tortworth
  ob.s.p.   d 1770
- Elizabeth Ducie = Francis Reynolds

Thomas Reynolds Moreton = Margaret Ramsden
2nd Lord Ducie of Tortworth
ob.s.p. d 1785

Francis Reynolds Moreton
= Mary Purvis

Thomas Reynolds Moreton = Francis, d of Earl of Caernarvon
1st Earl of Ducie
Baron Moreton of Tortworth
d. 1840

Henry George Francis = Elizabeth, d of 2nd Lord Sherborne
2nd Earl of Ducie
d 1853

SELECTED BIBLIOGRAPHY

Atkyns, *The Ancient & Present State of Gloucestershire (1712)*; Back, *The Story of Woodchester*; Beckinsale, *Companion into Gloucestershire*; Beresford & Joseph, *Mediaeval England*; Bibliotheca Gloucestrensis (1825); Burke, *Roman England*; Clayton, *Companion into Roman Britain*; Cavendish, *Prehistoric England*; Dictionary of National Biography; Ditchfield, *Memorials of Old Gloucestershire*; Dove, *The Story of Nympsfield*; Encyclopaedia Britannica; Fisher, *Notes & Recollections of Stroud (1891)*; Fuller, *Church History*; Grinsell, *The Ancient Burial Grounds of England*; Heighway, *Anglo Saxon Gloucestershire*; Hutton, *Highways & Byways of Gloucestershire*; Lloyd Baker, *The Story of Uley*; Lysons, *The Romans in Gloucestershire (1860)*; Mann, *The Cloth Industry in the West of England*; Martyn, *Egypt in Gloucestershire*; Mills & Riemer, *The Mills of Gloucestershire*; Morris & Moore, *Domesday Book Gloucestershire*; Murray, *Handbook of Glos, Hereford & Worcs (1872)*; Playne, *Minchinhampton & Avening*; Ponting, *The Woollen Industry of South West England*; Price, *The Normans in Gloucestershire & Bristol*; Rudder, *New History of Gloucestershire (1779)*; Ryder, *Gloucestershire through the Ages*; Scott-Giles, *The Road Goes On*; Smith & Ralph, *History of Bristol & Gloucestershire*; Tann, *Gloucestershire Woollen Mills*; Thurlow, *Osric*; Trevelyan, *English Social History*; Venn, *Foundations of Agricultural Economics (1923)*; Verey, *Gloucestershire: The Cotswolds*; Victoria County History, *Volumes X and XI*; White, *The Story of Gloucester*; Barlow, *Edward the Confessor*.

INDEX

References to photographs are given as PH 1–16. References to Nympsfield and the Smith family are not given for reasons of space and tidiness. Families are referred to by surname only.

Adelaide, South Australia 49
Adey 37, 38, 82
Alfred, King of Wessex 60
Alton Towers 56
Ambridge (The Archers) 46
Anthony, Saint 24, 26
Apsley, Lord 77
Archer-Shee, George 58
Armstrong, David 56, PH 14
Athelstan, King of England 27
Augustine, Saint 23
Aulus Plautius 72
Austin 71, 72, 74
Avening 21, 71, 73, 74

Bagendon 46
Baker 38
Balliol College, Oxford 56
Barberi, Dominic 49, 51, 55
Barry, Sir Charles 56
Bath 9, 19, 20, 25, 46, 76
Bell Court 46, 47, PH 12
Berkeley 1, 4, 8, 13, 28, 31, 32, 34, 36, 54, 61, 68, 73, 74
Bingham, Walter 40
Birmingham 39
Bisley 17
Black Death 71
Black Friars (Dominicans) 51, PH 10
Black Mountains 11, 80
Bodley, G.F. 70, 74
Boswell 59
Bown Hill 6, 11, 40, 41, PH 15
Breconshire Beacons 11, 80
Bristol 12, 34, 42, 68, 69
Bristol and Gloucestershire

Gliding Club 76, 77, 83
Brown 38, 82
Brown, Lancelot (Capability) 55
Buckholt Wood 6, 13, 20, 43, 63
Bucknell, Benjamin 56
Burford 37, 38, 51, 81, 82
Bushell 4, 37, 38, 82

Cam 15, 45, 72, 74
Canute, King of England 28
Cambridge (Glos) 40
Catholic Emancipation Act 50
Chadwick, Professor Owen 46
Chapel House PH 10
Charles I, King of England 42
Chaucer, Geoffrey 70
Cherington 21
Cirencester 9, 19, 21, 40, 44
Civil War 12
Claudia Ruffina 22, 23
Claudius, Emperor 15, 22
Clifford, Mrs E.M. 13
Clutterbuck 45
Coaley 10, 13
Coaley Peak 6, 9, 12–15, 20, 55, 62, 68, 80, 83, PH 2
Cobbett, William 63
Cockadilly 79, PH 6
Cole 38
Collins, Dr. Ray 66
Constantine III, Emperor 27
Court Farm 39, 47, 81, PH 6
Cromwell, Oliver 43
Crossland, Zoe 82
Crypt Grammar School 34

Dalby, L.J. 77

Dalgety Agriculture 40
Dangerfield 38
Daniels 4, 38, 39, 82
Davis 38
Deese, Maurice V.C. 58
Domesday Survey 21, 28, 30, 60, 68
Ducie, Earl of 47, 48, 50, 52, 54, 56, 62, 81
Ducie Moreton, Matthew 1st Lord 55, 63
Ducie, Sir Robert 54
Dursley 1, 4, 7, 8, 13, 15, 28, 31, 72, 78
Drabble, Margaret 7
Dyrham Park 27

Eastington 40
Easton, Ron 79
Ebley 1, 8, 71
Ebley Oil Mill 40, 41, 72
Edith, Queen of England 28
Edmund, King of England 27
Edward I 33
Edward II 32
Edward the Confessor 27, 28
Egypt Mill 40
Elizabeth I, Queen of England 34, 54
English Heritage 56
Estcourt 38
Evans, John PH 14

Fisher 82
Fitzharding, Robert 30
Fosse Way 9, 27
Frederick, Prince of Wales 55
Frocester 1, 9, 10, 13, 16, 19, 20, 43, 44, 54, 84
Fromehall Mill 74
Froude, R.H. & J.A. 48

Gatcombe Park 72
George II 55
George III 73
Gingell 38
Gloucester 9, 12, 19, 20, 22, 23, 25, 27, 28, 32, 42, 43, 45, 46, 67, 72
Godwin(e) Earl 20, 28
Goldingham, Major 11, 12, 16, PH 1
Gopsill Brown 69
Gracie, Capt. H.S. 16
Guinness, D 41
Guy Fawkes 37, 52
Gytha, Countess 20, 28

Hammond 38
Hansom, Charles 50, 51, 56
Hardy, Ann 56
Heaven 78
Henry I 30
Henry III 32, 45
Henry IV 33
Henry VIII 25, 33, 34 60
Hennessey, Prof 82
Herbert, Lord 43
Heskins 38
Hetty Pegler's Tump 6, 9, 12, 13, 24, 83
Hill 38
Hines 82
Hinton 38
Hodges 38, App A
Horsley 26, 73
Howell 4, 38
Huguenots 45
Huntingford Mill 72
Huntley, Sir George 54, 55, 61

Ireland 16, 18, 27, 67, 73
Isabella, Queen of England 32

James II 46, 47, PH 12
Jenner, Dr 73
John, King of England 32
Johnson, Dr Samuel 59

Keble, John & Rev Thomas 48
Kedwelly 38
Kelly, Reg 56
King 38, 40, 82

Kings School, Gloucester 34
Kingscote 45, 73
Kingstanley 1, 54, 57, 71, 73
Kingswood 73
Knight 38
Kinley 17, 20, 24, 25, 26, 34
Kyneburg, Abbess 25

Lee, Laurie 84
Lee, George 18
Leigh, William Snr., 47–52, 54–56
Leigh, William Jnr., 57
Leonard Stanley 1, 73
Lewis 38, 72
Linus 22
Lister, Dr. 73
Lister, R.A. & Cecil 41, 79
Little Aston (Staffs) 49, 51, 55
Lodgemore Mill 74
Longtree Hundred 13, 68

Magna Carta 32
Malmesbury 27
Malpass 45
Maris Convent and Chapel PH 9
Marling School 74, 82
Marling, Sir Percival, V.C. 11
Martyn, Marjorie 12
Massey, Sir Edward 42, 43
May Hill 11, 80
Metcalfe 54
Mills 4, 37, 38, 55, 78, 79, 81, 82
Mills, Kane 8, 34, 51, App A
Minchinhampton 17, 21, 63, 73
Morris, William 74

Nailsworth 1, 6, 9, 21, 60, 73
Neale 38, 81, 82
Newington Bagpath 45
Newman, Cardinal 48, 49, 51
Norris, J. 41
North Nibley 45
Notgrove 45

Oakridge 45
Orleans, Battle of 46

Osric, King of Hwicce 24, 25
Overton, Ann 82, PH 16
Owlpen 1, 73, 74, 83
Oxford Movement 48, 49

Park Mill 66, PH 14
Parsons 38
Pasteur, Dr Louis 73
Paine/Payne 38
Pearce/Pearse 38, 78
Pegler 12, 36–38, 81, 82
Penda, King of Mercia 24
Pitcher 78
Pomponia Graecina 22
Pope Gregory I 23
Pope Gregory XIII 45
Pope Pius IX 49, 52
Pope, Rev. Fr. Hugh 58
Preen 82
Price, E.G. & A. 16
Pucklechurch 27
Pugin, Augustus 48, 51, 56, 74
Pusey, Edward 48

Quakers 38
Quenington 67

Rank Hovis McDougal 39, 40
Rattigan, Sir Terence 58
Rayner, J. 83
Reform Act (1832) 48, 50
Repton, Humphrey 55
Reynolds, M. 81
Richard II 7, 33
Ridler, William Ridler 37
Rodborough 56
Rodman 82
Roger de Berkeley 28
Rose & Crown Inn 17, 47, 50, 70, 80, 81, PH 11
Rufus Pudens 22

St. Bartholomew's 40, 44, 45, 47, 72, 81, 82, PH 3, PH 4, PH 5
St. Joseph's 81–83
St. Margaret's 45, 46

91

Scotland 27
Scott, Sir George Gilbert 74
Scott, Sir Peter & Lady Phillipa 77
Selsley 6, 9, 19, 62, 71, 74, 83, 84
Shakespeare, William 7, 61
Shelton 4
Sheppard, Edward 71, 72
Shillam 38
Shipton Moyne 63
Silvester, Rev James 45, 79
Siseham 38
Smith Rogers & Co 40
Smiths Superfeed 41
Soldiers Grave 12, 14
Sparks 38
Spyer, John 55
Stephen, King of England 30
Stinchcombe 8
Stonehill 20, 80
Street Farm 47
Stroud District Council 56, 70, 83

Tacitus 22
Taylor 38
Teulon, S.S. 44, 47
Thames Head 17
Tinkley Farm 40
Tinkley Lane 9, 16
Toots (Selsley) 11, 12, 83
Townsend 4, 39, 81
Townsend, Viscount 63
Trevelyan, Prof. G.M. 34
Tull, Jethro 62, 63
Turtle 38
Tusser, Thomas 64
Tyndale, William 45

Uley Bury 6, 9–12, 15, 16, 19, 21, 62, 83
Uley 1, 12, 15, 17, 37, 45, 71–74, 83, 84, PH 8

Venn, Dr J.A. 68
Villiers, Capt. A.H. 54
Viollet-le-Duc, E-E, 56
Vizar, Arthur 7
Voltaire 62

Walkley 81
Watts 16, 79, 82
Waugh, Evelyn 81
Webb, Stephen 40
Wentworth Woodhouse 20
Westwood, Rose 56, 83, PH 16
Whitby, Synod of 25
White 82
Whitstone Hundred 13, 68
Whittington 46
William the Conqueror 28, 30
William Rufus 30
William, Rev 78, 79
Winstone 46
Wiseman, Cardinal 22, 49, 52
Woodchester 1, 19, 20, 28, 40, 50, 51, 54, 56, 58, 71, 74, 84, PH 7
Woodchester Park 6, 8, 12, 13, 44, 49, 50, 54–57, 61, 64, 66, 83, PH 13
Wooldridge 81
Worcester 25, 42, 67
Working Mens Club 84
Wotton under Edge 1, 31, 43, 71, 72
Wycliffe College 10